In Academia for the Church

Eastern and Central European Theological Perspectives

Edited by

Ábrahám Kovács

Zoltán Schwáb

Langham

MONOGRAPHS

© 2014 by Ábrahám Kovács and Zoltán Schwáb

Published 2014 by Langham Monographs
an imprint of Langham Creative Projects

Langham Partnership
PO Box 296, Carlisle,
Cumbria CA3 9WZ, UK
www.langham.org

ISBNs:
978-1-78368-946-0 Print
978-1-78368-944-6 Mobi
978-1-78368-945-3 ePub

British Library Cataloguing in Publication Data
In academia for the church.
 1. Church and college--Congresses. 2. Theology--Study and
 teaching (Higher)--Congresses.
 I. Kovács, Ábrahám editor. II. Schwáb, Zoltán S. editor.
 230'.071-dc23

 ISBN-13: 9781783689460

Cover & Book Design: projectluz.com

In Academia for the Church exhibits the far-reaching diversity of confessional and theological stances in East Central Europe where scholars agree that Christian theology must be pursued at its highest level. With this in mind the book addresses a challenging topic – how scholars in academia can and should relate their subject matter responsibly and earnestly to the needs of a wider Christian community. I highly recommend this volume for ministers, educators, theologians and laymen from Asia, Africa, the Americas, and Europe since the issues discussed in local context are truly global. The essays are thought-provoking, inviting the reader to further reflection and certainly evoking further discussions.

Professor Botond Gaál
Doctor of Hungarian Academy of Sciences
Debrecen Reformed Theological University, Hungary

In this volume the readers will be able to encounter the reflections of evangelical theologians from Eastern and Central Europe around the topic of *In Academia for the Church*. The papers aim to address the issues dialogically and challenge the contemporary ecclesial and academic life from different angles and by theologians deeply committed to the *missio Dei*. Important topics such as discipleship and spiritual formation, new dimensions of mission in the city or to minorities, and working at interdisciplinary fields have been engaged in a critical and constructive manner.

Tanya Petrova
Vice-rector for Academics
Bulgarian Evangelical Theological Institute, Sophia, Bulgaria

Theological colleges and Christian universities are a vital academic expression of the Kingdom of God, educationally empowering the people of God for the service of the church and society. Christian scholarship and academic excellence have to be viewed as part of biblical stewardship, and although the relationship between the Academy and Ecclesia does not exist without tensions, we must continually strive for creative balance, mutual accountability and respect in order to achieve optimal synergies and advance the performative dynamic of both. This diverse collection of East European contributions asks contextually relevant questions and points in the right direction.

Dr Peter Kuzmic
Eva B. and Paul E. Toms Distinguished Professor
of World Missions and European Studies
Gordon-Conwell Theological Seminary, USA

This collection is a rare gem. Ten theologians from Central and Eastern Europe set out to navigate the turbulent waters between the theological irrelevance and the theological pragmatism frequently found in the seminaries and theological institutes of Central and Eastern Europe. This book models a robust theological dialogue that points to the potential for transformed and transformative practices – those of the church in mission as well as those of the theological academy. Every theological educator intent on educating theological students in Central and Eastern Europe would be foolish not to read this book.

Rev Dr Darrell Jackson
Senior Lecturer in Missiology
Morling College, Sydney, Australia

CONTENTS

Listening to One Another!

Most evangelicals would agree that theological education should be in the service of the church. Such education aims to equip the church in order to fulfil God's purposes on earth. However, the reality on the ground does not always coincide with this stated agreement. A tension clearly exists between theological institutions and the church. In many cases theological institutions do not experience the assumed support of the church and the church does not feel that those institutions are preparing the right leadership for the church.

This is not the place to blame one or the other. What is urgently needed is genuine conversation where things are laid clearly and openly on the table awaiting us to work together by the Holy Spirit to bring mutual understanding and respect and to foster sincere reconciliation for the sake of the Kingdom. This book is a courageous attempt to set the table for a good conversation and to listen to one another.

John R. W. Stott has used the phrase 'double listening' urging us to listen both to the Word of God, and to today's world, in order to relate the one to the other. A similar process of 'double listening' is what theological institutions and churches need to engage in.

On 9 May 2012, I was delighted to accept the invitation of my two dear friends and veteran Langham scholars, Dr Ábrahám Kovács, Associate Professor of Dogmatics and Historical Theology at Debrecen Reformed Theological University, Debrecen, Hungary, and The Rev Prof Dr Parush R. Parushev, Doc Hab, Rector and Dean of Post-graduate Studies at the International Baptist Theological Seminary (Vrije Universiteit), Amsterdam, The Netherlands, to participate in a consultation in Berekfürdő, Hungary. The focus of the consultation was to explore the relationship between the academy and the church and to assert that the academy does exist to serve the church. This book is the product of that consultation. I am grateful to Langham Literature for publishing this book and thus contributing to a significant and successful attempt on the road of 'double listening'.

Although the articles of this book are addressed within a European context, the principles behind them along with the sensitivity and thoughtfulness in addressing the issues go beyond Europe. It is my prayer and hope that this book will encourage further discussion between the academy and the church to bring glory and honour to our Shepherd and Teacher.

Rev Riad Kassis, PhD
Director, Langham Scholars Ministry, Langham Partnership
International Director, International Council for Evangelical
Theological Education
Lebanon, 2014

Introduction

Theory and practice are believed to be the two sides of the same coin. Yet, one often finds theological educators who are 'one-sided'. Some scholars are so immersed in high-level academic discussions that their work hardly interacts with the main questions of the average churchgoer. Their students might feel that understanding the 'philosophical logic-chopper' of systematics and mastering the 'dead' languages of biblical studies does little service to their everyday life. One can also meet lecturers who err on the other side – theologians who might appear 'engaging' and 'relevant' to their students, but who compromise academic rigour, whose scholarship is dated, and whose methodology is dubious. Whichever form one-sidedness takes, a similar result ensues: it prevents theologians from presenting the good news with a powerful, credible voice.

Unfortunately, it is much easier to describe this one-sidedness in a brief paragraph than to avoid it in the messy realities of everyday practice. It is not only the case that combining relevance and academic rigour presents a methodological challenge. The spiritual challenge is not negligible either. Seeking popularity among students, or reputation in academic circles, or fame in secular society, can equally force scholars to give up their best aspirations towards balanced teaching.

The context of theological education explains many of the above-mentioned difficulties. When theologians investigate a doctrinal statement, an event in church history, or a biblical sentence, they rightly insist that it cannot be properly understood if they do not consider its context. However, while they explain this insight to their students, they themselves are working within a particular context: academia. In fact, this context often defines the language, conceptual categories, and aims of the teaching. At the same time, many of their academic theological institutions are intrinsically connected to, or even run by, Christian denominations and most of their students are preparing for different types of church service. An awareness of the details of this double contextual embeddedness of theological education (in academia and in church) is necessary for understanding its challenges.

Reflecting on the context of theological education highlights an additional complexity. Many of the younger generation of Eastern European theologians earned their PhDs in prestigious Western European universities. This certainly helps them to join cutting edge international academic discussions, but, at the same time, presents a serious question: how to apply their knowledge, obtained in the West, to the particular concerns of post-communist Eastern Europe?

Therefore, theological education is carried out in the overlapping segments of different contexts. Theologians have to negotiate between their loyalties to academia and to the church, and between the different concerns of Western and Eastern Europe at the very same time. This complex task resists easy solutions. On the contrary, it requires hard work, courage, and serious intellectual and spiritual attention. This is what prompted a group of Eastern European theologians to come together and think through some aspects of theological higher education. The result was the Second Langham Europe conference that took place in Berekfürdő, Hungary, in the spring of 2013.

One of the stimulating features of this conference was the sheer diversity of both the participants and their papers. Scholars came from many different countries (Bulgaria, Czech Republic, Croatia, England, Hungary, Romania, etc.), church background (Reformed, Baptist, Pentecostal, etc.), and disciplines (biblical studies, systematics, church history, pastoral theology, etc.). Yet, they had a common calling and passion that was appropriately captured by the title of the conference and this book: 'In Academia for the Church'.

The following selection of conference papers can be ordered into three groups. In the two essays in the first group, Old Testament scholar Tamás Czövek and New Testament scholar Ksenija Magda reflect, respectively, on the legacy of Johann Philipp Gabler and Rudolf Bultmann for theological education. Their interest is not purely antiquarian, however, but lies in how the thoughts of these eminent past theologians challenge contemporary practice in evangelical theological education. Then follows four essays that discuss how a special emphasis on postmodern concerns (Dóra Bernhardt), mission (András Lovas), moral responsibility (István Pásztori-Kupán), and public theology (Tamás Béres) can re-invigorate theological education. The final group is comprised of the studies of four theologians who fulfil important leadership roles in higher education within their Lutheran (Tibor Fabiny), Pentecostal (Corneliu Constantineanu), and Baptist (Corneliu C. Simut, Parush R. Parushev) contexts. They reflect on the relationship between theology and universities and on the role Christianity can play in higher education institutions.

The reader will recognize that the authors of these essays do not always agree on every point, which is surely a strength, and not a weakness, of the collection. These diverse, occasionally contradicting, viewpoints will hopefully stimulate the reader to reflect further and to continue the friendly debates of the conference. We hope and pray that this will lead to a theological education that is academically robust but which also enriches the church.

Ábrahám Kovács and Zoltán Schwáb
Edinburgh-Durham, January, 2014

CHAPTER 1

History and Theology: Johann Philipp Gabler's Legacy in Biblical Studies

Tamás Czövek

When the scientific discoveries of the modern era were shaking the foundations of the medieval worldview like the Ptolemaic system, a literal interpretation of the Bible, and with the precritical worldview giving way to a scientific or modern one, the decisive battle of theology was fought between the conservatives, intent on upholding the age-old doctrines of the church, and the neologists, who tried to accommodate the historical efforts to the new scientific scenery and, at the same time, salvaging theology or some tenets of faith, at least.[1] So it was in the heyday of the Enlightenment, in the year 1777, that the famous German philosopher, Gotthold Ephraim Lessing, despaired of seeing a resolution to this dilemma of history and theology and thought of them as an either-or scenario.[2] His famous sentence refers to this dichotomy between history and theology: "That, then, is the ugly great ditch which I cannot cross, however often and however earnestly I have tried to make that leap." Lessing's despair is

---

1. On liberal theology's intent on salvaging theology, see R. Morgan and J. Barton, *Biblical Interpretation*, OBS (Oxford: OUP, 1988).

2. The third pillar of biblical studies is the literary aspect posing problems of another kind than those discussed here.

a fitting reminder of the era's quandary: Is history to be chosen instead of theology or rather is theology to be preferred over against history?[3]

Johann Philipp Gabler

On one side of Lessing's ditch camped Protestant orthodox theology with its high claims to church doctrines, allegedly all based on the Bible. On the opposite side stood a growing number of neologist theologians discontent with both the authoritarian attitude of church theology as well as the proof-texting method and assertions unsubstantiated, in their view, in the Bible. The neologists' critique, whose main concern was the historical point of reference of biblical texts, was that historically the biblical texts could not claim what they were supposed or thought to claim by the conservatives.

With the concerted attacks of neologists on orthodox Protestantism events gathered momentum and, 10 years after Lessing's statement, reached the point of no return. Ever since Johann Philipp Gabler's influential inaugural address "On the right differentiation between biblical and dogmatic theology and on the correct drawing of the boundaries of each" at Altdorf University in 1787, biblical studies have been different and, at the same time, in a different predicament than before.[4] Gabler saw

---

3. I am not claiming that it was Lessing who first tried to tackle the dilemma of history or theology which certainly goes back to antiquity. Whether or not historically true, the famous note by Clement of Alexandria on the authorship of John's Gospel can be read in these terms. Eusebius (*H.E.* 6.14.7) quotes Clement, "But that John, last of all, conscious that the outward facts had been set forth in the Gospels, was urged on by his disciples, and, divinely moved by the Spirit, composed a spiritual Gospel;" cited by D. A. Carson, D. J. Moo, and L. Morris, *An Introduction to the New Testament* (Leicester: Apollos, 1992), p. 140. The 'outward facts' I take to refer to the historical while the 'spiritual' is the theological. These two sides of the coin can be seen in contemporary readings where John's Gospel is deemed less historical than the synoptics. On the other hand, popular piety has valued the gospel for its more straightforward theology (i.e. more 'spiritual' Christology and soteriology) than that of the synoptics.

4. One of the main questions, not only of this consultation but of theological education in general, is how academia can serve the church. The problem prior to Gabler's lecture was dogmatics keeping a tight rein on biblical studies, church on academia. With Gabler's call for proper distinction of theological disciplines, biblical studies have increasingly been given full rein over church doctrines, resulting in the emancipation of the former. I am not claiming that the situation in church and academia had been any better up to that point. Gabler's oration set the record straight in one respect only to introduce another set

biblical studies (what he called biblical theology) consisting of historical investigation into the beliefs of the biblical authors as presented in the text. As he put it, "There is truly a biblical theology, of historical origin, conveying what the holy writers felt about divine matters." "That being the case," he goes on,

> it is necessary, unless we want to labour uselessly, to distinguish among each of the periods in the Old and New Testaments, each of the authors, and each of the manners of speaking which each used as a reflection of time and place, whether these manners are historical or didactic or poetic. [. . .] Therefore we must carefully collect and classify each of the ideas of each patriarch – Moses, David, and Solomon, and of each prophet with special attention to Isaiah, Jeremiah, Ezekiel, Daniel, Hosea, Zachariah, Haggai, Malachi, and the rest; and for many reasons we ought to include the apocryphal books for this same purpose; also we should include the ideas from the epoch of the New Testament, those of Jesus, Paul, Peter, John, and James. Above all, this process is completed in two ways: the one is in the legitimate interpretation of passages pertinent to this procedure; the other is in the careful comparison of the ideas of all the sacred authors among themselves.

Gabler's concluding sentence sums up his thesis.

> Thus the manner and form of dogmatic theology should be varied, as Christian philosophy especially is, according to the variety both of philosophy and of every human point of view of that which is subtle, learned, suitable and appropriate, elegant and graceful; biblical theology itself remains the same, namely in that it deals only with those things which holy men

---

of difficulties. But then it is dilemmas and predicaments we have to live with.

perceived about matters pertinent to religion, and is not made
to accommodate our point of view.[5]

In short, for Gabler biblical studies were historic in character and therefore
constant. Texts, in his view, should be interpreted with reference to their
historic circumstances. He therefore assigned to biblical studies the rather
descriptive task of the theology of the Bible and related tasks of linguistics,
philology, exegesis and the like. On the other hand, by not being dependent
on the historical circumstances, 'dogmatic theology' concerns itself with
what should be believed, therefore normative. The particular characteristics
of both need to be kept in mind when operating them.

Essential as all these operations were, in due time they led to a mode of
investigation in biblical studies that is void of theology. For this reason, the
term 'biblical theology' was early used to combat this mode. Thus Gabler's
program has had a double effect: 1) by furthering biblical studies as defined
by him it has in fact driven a wedge between biblical and theological studies;
2) this alienation has made those conscious of the theological character of
the Bible and the need of a *theological* study endeavor to study the Bible
more in terms of theology.[6]

On the one hand, biblical studies are supposed to concern themselves
with events, cultures, persons – data of antiquity. On the other, they are,
particularly when taught in the context of church, expected to address
current questions of politics, society, culture and science – present questions.
How do we do this double duty? How do we succeed in bridging the gap? I
do not have the final answer. Certainly there are good examples that balance
history and religion well. In what follows I will try to portray the situation
by analyzing some publications and representatives of biblical studies I
consider one-sided (i.e. being on either side of Lessing's ugly ditch).

---

5. As translated by J. Sandys-Wunsch and L. Eldredge, "J. P. Gabler and the Distinction
between Biblical and Dogmatic Theology: Translation, Commentary, and Discussion of
His Originality," *SJT*, 33 (1980), 133–44 (pp. 137, 139–140, 144).
6. J. Barr, *The Concept of Biblical Theology: An Old Testament Perspective* (London: SCM,
1999), pp. 6–8.

Biblical Studies Void of Theology

As Chesterton is often quoted as saying, "The whole modern world has divided itself into conservatives and progressives. The business of progressives is to go on making mistakes. The business of conservatives is to prevent the mistakes from being corrected." Risking an oversimplification, this seems to have been realized in biblical studies, the progressives being those keen on history and the conservatives concerned with theology.

Commentaries inevitably discuss historical, grammatical, philological and exegetical questions.[7] These discussions may or may not lead to theology. Examples of exegetical discussions not leading to theology abound. The East-German *Theologischer Handkommentar zum Neuen Testament* series are strong on philological details and exegesis but rather weak on theology. The interpretation of John 21:1–14 by Johannes Schneider only touches on theological questions when discussing the 153 fish, the motif of the untorn net and the statement in 21:12 ("None of the disciples dared ask him, 'Who are you?' They knew it was the Lord" (NIV)), but, in my view, does not make sufficient effort to deal with them.[8] Schneider often just paraphrases the narrative which at times is helpful, other times, however, sounds rather boring.

Several volumes of the *Word Biblical Commentary* series can be taken as another example of divorcing theology from biblical studies. It leaves room for theological reflection but contributors do not or cannot pay sufficient attention to this. The discussion of John 21 conforms to the series structure of 'Translation' (1 page) followed by 'Notes' (1 page), 'Form/Structure/ Setting' (3 pages), 'Comment' (the bulk of the discussion; 18 pages) and 'Explanation' (2 pages) which is the most theologically focused part. This

---

7. Exegesis or theological study of the Bible is conventionally thought to "denote a historical analysis of the religious terminology and concepts of the Old Testament texts in relation to their world of origin." As opposed to this understanding, exegesis or theological commentary is concerned with "the meaning of the Old Testament texts in relation to Christian faith as a living reality." W. L. Moberly, "What is Theological Commentary? An Old Testament Perspective," in R. M. Allen, *Theological Commentary: Evangelical Perspectives* (Bloomsbury: T & T Clark, 2011, 172–186), p. 173.

8. J. Schneider, *Das Evangelium nach Johannes*, THKNT (Berlin: Evangelische Verlagsanstalt, 1976), pp. 330–331. Some of the other commentaries in the series are even less theological.

structure is helpful and makes the discussion transparent. Apparently, however, it is up to the reader to extract more theology from the analysis. George R. Beasley-Murray discusses theological themes like the apostles' call, the fellowship meal on the seashore, Christian leadership, Peter over against the beloved disciple and the example of the beloved disciple. Of these, only the seashore meal is specifically related to the chapter.[9] In addition, questions to which answers could be expected, like "Why did Jesus appear in this way (see 21:1, 14)?" or "Why did the disciples not dare ask Jesus who he was?" or "How was such a *symposion* judged by the first audience?" or "How does this episode conclude the story begun in chapter 1?" he leaves untouched. In the editors' words, WBC "seeks to make the technical and scholarly approach to a theological understanding of Scripture understandable by – and useful to – the fledgling student, the working minister as well as to colleagues in the guild of professional scholars and teachers." One wonders whether this purpose of rendering a theological understanding of Scripture has been achieved to the highest possible extent.[10]

A third example of biblical studies in Gabler's style, another interpretation of John 21:1–14, is that of Don Carson. He too provides helpful linguistic and exegetical notes, explains the background, sequence of actions as well as the scene and carefully considers various interpretations. Still, the net theological yield is rather meager when Carson concerns himself with the theological themes of the apostles' call, the number 153 and the import of 21:12, quoted above.[11]

Theology is also neglected in many Old and New Testament introductions. Conservative scholarship has considered questions of authorship and date as a showcase to prove the reliability of Scripture. In this fashion Gleason L. Archer has extensively argued for the Mosaic authorship of the Pentateuch

---

9. The relationship of Peter and the beloved disciple first features in chapter 13.

10. G. R. Beasley-Murray, *John*, WBC, 36 (Waco: Word Books, 1987), pp. 392–418 and ix.

11. D. A. Carson, *The Gospel According to John* (Leicester–Grand Rapids: IVP–Eerdmans, 1991), pp. 668–675. To be fair to Beasley-Murray and Carson, one of their purposes possibly was to demonstrate that the biblical account is reliable. This might be one of the underlying reasons of historical questions being pushed in the foreground at the cost of theology.

as well as an early, mid-fifteenth century date of the exodus. In discussing the conquest he refers to John Garstang's excavation of Jericho in the 1930s but, even though his book was first published in 1964, fails to mention Kathleen Kenyon's digging in the 1950s that has led to a revision of the city's history (and that of the conquest).[12] It is an untenable position that shows a double standard in doing biblical scholarship as well as the difficulty of prioritizing certain theological-apologetic aspects over against history. But more importantly and to the point of our subject matter, assuming that Archer is right, one wonders what theological significance an early dating of the conquest or a Mosaic authorship has. Despite the polemic attitude and the mass of data Archer presents, he is not forthcoming in this respect.

Péter Balla, the renowned New Testament scholar of Károli University in Budapest, published a New Testament introduction in 2005.[13] I sent him my observations in a personal communication the following year. My critique was positive while questioning some aspects. Here are two of my comments.

> Conventionally, introductions are investigations in the fields of biblical studies with little theological relevance. For this very reason, it has come under attack in the last 35 years or so and gone through some major modifications.[14] You do refer to canonical criticism and Brevard Childs – your bibliography lists three of his works. Obviously, you are interested in the New Testament aspects of Childs' work. His 1979

---

12. G. L. Archer, *A Survey of Old Testament Introduction* (Chicago: Moody, 1994). I refer to the Hungarian edition; *Az ószövetségi bevezetés vizsgálata* (Budapest: KIA, 2001), pp. 135–145, 265, 273–274; cf. W. G. Dever, *Who Were the Early Israelites and Where Did They Come From?* (Grand Rapids: Eerdmans, 2003), pp. 45–47. As a matter of fact, Kenyon goes unnoticed in Archer's index.

13. P. Balla, *Az újszövetségi iratok és kanonikus gyűjteményük kialakulásának története (Bevezetéstani alternatívák)* (Budapest: KRE HTK, 2005).

14. Here I want to refer to two critical and theological Old Testament introductions: W. Brueggemann, *An Introduction to the Old Testament: The Canon and Christian Imagination* (Louisville: Westminster John Knox, 2003); D. M. Carr, *An Introduction to the Old Testament: Sacred Texts and Imperial Contexts of the Hebrew Bible* (Chichester: Wiley-Blackwell, 2010). I should also mention B. S. Childs, *Introduction to the Old Testament as Scripture* (Philadelphia: Fortress, 1979). His introduction, however, is not theological to the extent he aspires it to be; see also the criticism of Barr, *Concept*, pp. 394–395.

Introduction to the OT as Scripture, however, has an extensive discussion of why he deems conventional introductions, from the perspective of theology, unsatisfactory. In my view, by including this aspect in your discussion you could have made it more fraught with theology as well as slightly more relevant to the education of future pastors.

And,

I think, regarding the present consensus, it is refreshing to read a conservative introduction like yours and realize that a conservative point of view does not necessarily mean a head-in-the-sand attitude. What kept cropping up, however, in my mind when reading claims like "the authorship of John/Matthew is tenable" was, well, we have considered the arguments for Johannine/Matthean origin – what is the theological significance of all this? Of course I interpret the book differently if it dates from the middle of the first century than if it dates from the early second century. Is it, however, a mere epistemological/historical conclusion or does authorship have any theological import? Among others Northrop Frye has emphasized the fact that most biblical books are anonymous. Therefore a claim to authority is based on content rather than origin.

In this respect, there does not seem to be an essential difference between conservative and non-conservative biblical scholarship. Indeed, this mode of investigation is the consistent realization of Gabler's programme, for good and bad.

Biblical Studies Void of History

It is not anti-intellectualism but a disenchantment with historical criticism, that "locked the Bible into the past," that is the driving force of pursuing theological interpretations.[15] I will name two Old Testament scholars I otherwise much respect who are disillusioned with historical criticism. First, Brevard Childs who was instrumental in the emergence of canonical criticism, a corrective to the historical-critical approach. However, the uneasy relationship between the history of religion approach and theology is too clear in Childs' approach. As James Barr notes, it can be seen as implying an attempt to expel all influence of the history of religion from biblical interpretation. There is Scripture itself, and there is theology; theological interpretation is done direct from Scripture, and there is no intermediary, since any intermediary would break down the sole dependence on the canonical form of Scripture, which alone is authoritative for theology.[16]

The section on 'Theological Reflection' in Childs' Exodus commentary "attempts to build on the previous exegetical and historical work of the commentary, and to develop a more rigorous method of actualizing the text for the church's present task", an aspect "either missing or attached as an unrelated appendix to critical exegesis".[17] Reading the reflections, however, one feels let down so that Barr seems correct when claiming that the chapter "does not amount to much – just the same fault which had been blamed on the inadequate theological character of previous commentaries."[18] Similar things can be said of Childs' *Biblical Theology* – it is less theological than could be expected.[19] In brief, Childs' approach is a result of his insistence on theology with history thrown out and sneaking in through the back door.

My second example is Walter Brueggemann, the Old Testament scholar who has made every effort to make the Bible speak in its own right. All his publications are fruits of this theological endeavor. When compared with Childs, an interesting difference can be seen. While Childs often attacks

---

15. The words are those of another advocate of canonical criticism, J. A. Sanders, *Canon and Community: A Guide to Canonical Criticism* (Philadelphia: Fortress, 1984), p. 5.

16. J. Barr, *Holy Scripture: Canon, Authority, Criticism* (Oxford: OUP, 1983), p. 94. This criticism by Barr may seem one-sided to some.

17. B. S. Childs, *The Book of Exodus: A Critical, Theological Commentary*, OTL (Louisville: Westminster, 1974), p. xvi.

18. Barr, *Concept*, p. 393.

19. B. S. Childs, *Biblical Theology of the Old and New Testaments: Theological Reflection on the Christian Bible* (Minneapolis: Fortress, 1992).

historical criticism head-on, Brueggemann is more amicable towards it. Still, Childs makes use of historical-critical results in his *Biblical Theology* or Exodus commentary to a much higher extent than does Brueggemann in his *Theology of the Old Testament* or Genesis commentary.[20] Thus Barr appreciates Brueggemann's openness "to various trends of scholarship" while expressing astonishment at his rejection of the historical method. I think, however, that Barr exaggerates when seeing Brueggemann as "extremely negative towards historical criticism."[21] In my estimate, Brueggemann is simply discontent with the method and its results and jettisons it, along with history, from his methodology: historical criticism has not only not delivered but (realizing Gabler's programme) resulted in a genetic, historical, text-critical, philological (i.e. non-theological) mode of operation. At any rate, to read lines by Brueggemann like, "The gains of historical criticism are immense, and no informed reader can proceed without paying attention to those gains" and at the same time seeing his ahistorical Old Testament theology is perplexing.[22] In his attempt to let the Bible speak for itself it is the more confusing to see biblical history disappear to the effect that Barr correctly claims that in Brueggemann's ahistorical Old Testament theology there are no people and nothing happens. He also criticizes Brueggemann for using a preaching, homiletic style, of which his extravagant rhetoric is characteristic, instead of reasoning with arguments.[23] Theology has won the day and history lost.

Turning to popular theological, also known as spiritual literature, we can observe that history plays an even less significant role in it than in the academic works of Childs and Brueggemann. Grass-roots church piety seldom sees the point of academic questions and investigations. They view themselves or the church as not benefiting from this endeavour. The church, in former Communist countries in particular, has managed to thrive without this after all, so why bother with these academic and intellectual questions? However, by bracketing history out, or relinquishing the

---

20. W. Brueggemann, *Theology of the Old Testament: Testimony, Dispute, Advocacy* (Minneapolis: Fortress, 1997); *Genesis*, Interpretation (Atlanta: John Knox, 1982).

21. Barr, *Concept*, p. 545.

22. Brueggemann, *Theology*, p. 14.

23. Barr, *Concept*, pp. 558–559, 545–549.

sometimes unbearable but fruitful tension of history and theology, biblical studies are in danger of becoming anachronistic and therefore irrelevant.[24]

Don Carson gives a summary of four stages of theological interpretation:

> At the first level, the Bible must be understood exegetically, within its literary and historical contexts, with appropriate attention devoted to literary genre, attempting to unfold authorial intent so far as it is disclosed in the text. At level 2, the text must be understood within the whole of biblical theology, including where it fits into and what it contributes to the unfolding storyline and its theology. At level 3, the theological structures found in the text are brought to bear upon, and understood in concert with, other major theological emphases derived from Scripture. At level 4, all teachings derived (or ostensibly derived) from the biblical text are subjected to and modified by a larger hermeneutical proposal (e.g. Trinitarian action, God's love and freedom, or something vague such as "what was disclosed in Jesus").[25]

Even though level 4 appears to operate in the pre-Gabler framework these guidelines demonstrate an awareness of the need and difficulties of theological interpretation. I think along these lines we can start to develop a theological interpretation not void of history.

Concluding Remarks

I do not have the final answer. At best I perceive the pitfalls and fallacies without necessarily knowing how exactly to do it right. We should bear in

---

24. I am not advocating an exclusively historical approach, since some modes of biblical studies like structuralism and rhetorical criticism are valid and valuable approaches to the text.

25. D. A. Carson, "Theological Interpretation of Scripture: Yes, But . . . ," in R. M. Allen, *Theological Commentary: Evangelical Perspectives* (Bloomsbury: T & T Clark, 2011, 187–207), p. 207.

mind that, by definition, theology is not descriptive – it is the food of the church. Biblical scholars do not take popular theological literature seriously, for obvious reasons, and popular theologians fail to interact with academic theology. Whether right or wrong, however, in this way this alienation by both parties has contributed to an antagonism of church and academia. Barr's warning of a church ruling supreme should be taken to heart: "It is in the interest of the believing community itself that it should not too jealously insist on keeping the interpretation of Scripture, and indeed theological education altogether, within the control of its own hands."[26] The other side is equally important: the seminary should be in touch with the outside world and, in particular, with the church in order to avoid an ivory-tower mentality and a scholarship irrelevant to church life.

It is difficult to achieve a biblical theology based on or, in some way, related to history; the demise of the biblical theology movement warns us of this fact. But Christianity, whether or not a religion of timeless truths, is said to be a historical religion.[27] So how do we reconcile history and theology? If taken to relate to seminary education, George Mendenhall's statement of half a century ago is relevant to our question: "Biblical theology divorced from historical reality ends in a kind of ritual docetism, and history apart from religious value is a valueless secularized hobby of antiquarians."[28]

Bibliography

Archer, G. L. *A Survey of Old Testament Introduction*. Chicago: Moody, 1994.

Balla, P. *Az újszövetségi iratok és kanonikus gyűjteményük kialakulásának története (Bevezetéstani alternatívák)*. Budapest: KRE HTK, 2005.

Barr, J. *Explorations in Theology 7, The Scope and Authority of the Bible*. London: SCM, 1980.

———. *Holy Scripture: Canon, Authority, Criticism*. Oxford: OUP, 1983.

---

26. J. Barr, *Explorations in Theology 7, The Scope and Authority of the Bible* (London: SCM, 1980), p. 123.

27. On this see Barr, *Explorations*, pp. 30–35.

28. G. Mendenhall, "The Hebrew Conquest of Palestine," BA, (1962), 65–87, (p. 74).

―――. *The Concept of Biblical Theology: An Old Testament Perspective.* London: SCM, 1999.

Beasley-Murray, G. R. *John*, WBC, 36. Waco: Word Books, 1987

Brueggemann, W. *Genesis*, Interpretation. Atlanta: John Knox, 1982.

―――. *Theology of the Old Testament: Testimony, Dispute, Advocacy.* Minneapolis: Fortress, 1997.

―――. *An Introduction to the Old Testament: The Canon and Christian Imagination.* Louisville: Westminster John Knox, 2003.

Carson, D. A. *The Gospel According to John.* Leicester–Grand Rapids: IVP–Eerdmans, 1991.

―――. "Theological Interpretation of Scripture: Yes, But . . ." in R. M. Allen, *Theological Commentary: Evangelical Perspectives.* Bloomsbury: T & T Clark, 2011, 187–207.

Carson, D. A.; D. J. Moo, and L. Morris. *An Introduction to the New Testament.* Leicester: Apollos, 1992.

Carr, D. M. *An Introduction to the Old Testament: Sacred Texts and Imperial Contexts of the Hebrew Bible.* Chichester: Wiley-Blackwell, 2010.

Childs, B. S. *The Book of Exodus: A Critical, Theological Commentary*, OTL. Louisville: Westminster, 1974.

―――. *Introduction to the Old Testament as Scripture.* Philadelphia: Fortress, 1979.

―――. *Biblical Theology of the Old and New Testaments: Theological Reflection on the Christian Bible.* Minneapolis: Fortress, 1992.

Dever, W. G. *Who Were the Early Israelites and Where Did They Come From?* Grand Rapids: Eerdmans, 2003.

Mendenhall, G. "The Hebrew Conquest of Palestine", *Biblical Archaeologist, 25*, (1962): 65–87.

Moberly, W. L., "What is Theological Commentary? An Old Testament Perspective," in R. M. Allen, *Theological Commentary: Evangelical Perspectives.* Bloomsbury: T & T Clark, 2011, 172–186.

Morgan, R. and J. Barton. *Biblical Interpretation*, OBS. Oxford: OUP, 1988.

Sanders, J. A. *Canon and Community: A Guide to Canonical Criticism.* Philadelphia: Fortress, 1984.

Sandys-Wunsch, J. and L. Eldredge, "J. P. Gabler and the Distinction between Biblical and Dogmatic Theology: Translation, Commentary, and Discussion of His Originality", *SJT, 33*, (1980): 133–44.

Schneider, J. *Das Evangelium nach Johannes*, THKNT. Berlin: Evangelische Verlagsanstalt, 1976.

CHAPTER 2

Should Theological Academic Environments Be More Spiritually Formative and Practical?

Ksenija Magda

Today, evangelical theological education cannot be imagined without spiritual formation courses, while conferences on theological education deal with the mandatory question: *how* can academic environments be additionally, or even primarily, spiritually formative? Since I officially entered the debate in 2002 at the Baptist International Conference on Theological Education (BICTE) in Seville, and obviously even before that, this 'how' has been argued back and forth. Spirituality is, by perception, a necessity for future theologians.

Arthur Holmes, for instance, in his investigation of the values of a Christian academy as an institution, points to four 'recurring emphases' in theological education: the usefulness of the liberal arts as preparation for service in both church and society; the unity of truth; contemplative (or doxological) learning; and the care of the soul (what we call moral and spiritual formation).[1] He proves his point by giving biblical examples for the first three, but concludes that the 'care of the soul is obvious'.[2] This fourth point means that students of theology need to learn to adhere to

---

1. Arthur Holmes, *Building the Christian Academy* (Grand Rapids: Eerdmans, 2001), p. 2.
2. "Along with the broad uses learning serves". Holmes, p. 5.

certain standards 'for moral character and faith development'.[3] However, while I agree that moral character should be a prerequisite for all human activity, I have reservations about the 'concern for faith development'. In my experience, this often means the fine-tuning of new academics to a set of doctrines.[4] It follows that spirituality is often assessed against the doctrinal demands of a particular denomination, which hinders academic discussions.

Laudably, *The Cape Town Commitment* urges evangelicals instead to ensure "that institutions and programmes of theological education conduct a missional audit of their curricula, structures and ethos, to ensure that they truly serve the needs and opportunities facing the church in their cultures".[5] This concept sounds familiar enough to evangelical ears, but in fact, it is not. Instead of being directed towards the needs of the church, this document focuses on the "opportunities facing the church in their cultures". Consequently, it also demands "the Bible at the centre" rather than denominational doctrine as the core theological activity. Evangelical theological education institutions should address the study of the Bible as their core discipline. Although this may be perceived as ordinary evangelical rhetoric, I believe that the attempt to practice it would be revolutionary. The document suggests that the main criterion for successful spiritual formation is the candidate's ability to adjust to the needs and opportunities *outside* the church. Thus the study of the Bible, instead of doctrine, becomes the core activity of students.

However, if this is what the theological academic world is called to do, then we encounter a two-fold problem, which is no novelty. On the one hand, we need to define the relationship between 'missional' and 'academic'; and on the other, we need to define what it really means to 're-centre the study of the Bible as a core discipline' – in other words, we have arrived

---

3. Ibid.

4. For instance, some evangelical schools will promote "no women in ministry; no charismata; no ecumenism" as necessary for formation. Some schools may require signing of a creed regularly.

5. D. Birdsall and L. Brown, eds., *The Cape Town Commitment.* http://www.lausanne.org/en/documents/ctcommitment.html#p2-6 accessed 9 May 2013.

at a point of discussing the scope and methodology of biblical theology in relation to dogmatics.

The first challenge is to describe the task of academia in general and within it, theological academia. The task of academia is to evaluate and re-evaluate traditions and critically dissect them to prove or disprove their value – to tear them apart and test the stuff of which they are made. If this is so, all science and humanities, and theology in particular, have a place in these processes. But if it can be agreed that theological academic excellence is necessary in evaluating and re-evaluating theological traditions, should we in any sense expect the doctrinal and missional formation of academics to happen in theological institutions, especially if spirituality is defined by doctrine? Should spirituality not be defined differently to fit all Christian endeavours, including theological academia? If so, it cannot be developed by adhering to proven doctrines, by burdening the curriculum with spirituality courses, or by insisting that theological academics should be more down-to-earth and practical. Certain sympathies can be developed for such pious sticking plasters, treating what I would call the major trauma of the last century's peak in secularization and the challenges to faith which hit the church. But I am not sure this is helping the church to recover from her deep injuries.

I propose that the problem be observed from a different angle according to which theological academia is not held responsible for the 'useless' ministers of the twentieth century in the West. There are several examples that could be used, but I suggest that in our next section we turn to the Tübingen school which, at least in our region, has served as a paradigm for unholy theological studies, and to Rudolf Bultmann, its leading and most controversial character. After this I will make some more general comments about the state of evangelical theological education in Croatia to contribute to the first question on the task of theological academia. Only after this I will address the request of how to re-centre theology around biblical studies.

The Task of Theological Academia

If Helmut Thielicke is right in his evaluation of Rudolf Bultmann as expressed in his memoirs *Zu Gast auf einem schönen Stern,* Bultmann claimed for decades that his peers misunderstood him.[6] According to Thielicke and also Karl Jaspers, Bultmann's greatest problem was academic stubbornness. Jaspers allegedly said of him: "*Er lernt nichts hinzu. Keine Kritik hat jemals irgendeine Revision bei ihm ausgelöst. Er sitzt fest wie eine fensterlose Monade im Gehäuse seiner Terminologie.*"[7] (He comes to no new learning. No criticism ever triggers a revision in him. He sits firm in his windowless tower, in the solid shell of his terminology.) This is an extremely distressing evaluation of a theologian whose 'starting points' were that the "forms of expression are inevitably bound to temporal imaginations and terminology", and that "such time-confined terms cannot be the object of our faith".[8] These evaluations, one by a contemporary and the other by a student of Bultmann's, show that Bultmann too (to use a German saying) only 'cooked with water' when it came to theology.

However, as often, the picture is not entirely black and white. As I argue shortly, Bultmann was not an entirely narrow-minded scholar, as the above few lines might suggest. Neither was he an ardent enemy of the church, as later evangelical rhetoric often presents him.

Bultmann, just like many of his contemporaries, was scared of Bible critics who dissected Christianity historically and displayed it as a historical fraud. However, he wrote to Barth: "In my view, dogmatics must have the coming generations in mind in relation to both pastors and congregations. What are the thoughts that live today behind our educated people and in our papers? Must theology always arrive after the event?"[9] In other words, for him, useful dogmatics would go beyond a 'faithful repetition'

---

6. Thielicke, *Zu Gast auf einem schönen Stern: Erinnerungen* (Hamburg: Hoffmann und Campe, 1986), p. 172. For instance, Bultmann wrote to Barth; "You do not understand what I am after in my book." B. Jaspert, *Karl Barth – Rudolf Bultmann: Letters 1922–1966* (Edinburgh: T & T Clark, 1982) p. 28.

7. Ibid., p. 173.

8. Ibid., p. 172.

9. Jaspert, *Barth/Bultmann*, p. 39.

of old dogmatic formulations. Instead, he was seeking how to engage directly with the burning problems of the 'coming generations.' Maybe his concern for unchurched academia made him less ready to reflect on his own proposals critically enough. He tried to enter the academic argument because he saw no way around it. He disapproved of what he thought was Barth's uncritical devotion to certain dogmas. "I am sorry that you do not enter into critical debate with your friends . . . What is more important is that you have failed to enter into (latent but radical) debate with modern philosophy and have naively adopted the older ontology from patristic and scholastic dogmatics."[10]

Bultmann recognized that something new was happening to academia which required a re-evaluation of method and even of the old dogmatic language of the church. John MacQuarrie analyses it thus: "Bultmann does recognize the dangers that arise if Christian thought is isolated from the general thinking of our time . . . he asks how the Christian message can be heard and understood if the stress on its distinctiveness is allowed to lead to its encapsulation."[11] For Bultmann, existentialism did offer some new solutions, after all, there are things in the past which transcend history and become the story of all people. Apparently he wrote of Heidegger's *Sein und Zeit,* "I attained a deeper understanding of the historical character of human existence, and thereby at the same time of the conceptual framework in which theology too can operate in order to bring faith to appropriate expression as an existential attitude."[12] The Bible contains such timeless truths.

Can we blame Bultmann for his inability to pinpoint then and there the relationship between the historical 'shell' and 'timeless' core? This problem, as Thielicke predicted 30 years ago, has proven surprisingly resistant and outlived him.[13] But his solution, the 'demythologization' of the Bible, has not. Rather, it has gained him an awkward reputation among doctrinally orthodox church elements, overshadowing his otherwise brilliant exegetical

---

10. Jaspert, *Barth/Bultmann*, p. 38.
11. John Macquarrie, "Philosophy and Theology in Bultmann's Thought" in Charles W. Kegley, ed. *The Theology of Rudolf Bultmann* (New York: Harper & Row, 1966), pp. 128–129.
12. As quoted in Macquirre, "Philosophy and Theology", p. 129.
13. Thielicke, p. 172.

insights. Bultmann has become the paradigm of liberalism and has played into the hands of people whose experience of faith he intended to safeguard against secularization. Barth, on the other hand, played it safe. To this day, he is a much loved, relatively uncontroversial (with regards to orthodoxy) scholar. However, it seems to me that he is also a paradigm for orthodox Christianity's avoidance of trauma. His *opus magnum* is revealingly named *Dogmatics* – and it seems to me that while Bultmann tried to tackle the intricacies of Modernity, Barth was hesitant to look outside the dogmatic fort. His letters reveal his constant withdrawal from discussions, even to the point of blaming himself (cynically or truthfully, I cannot decide) for a lack of further academic capacity. He answers Bultmann's objections, "I doubt whether it will be possible even to come close to satisfying you, because what you want of me finally amounts to no more and no less than an alteration of the intellectual *habitus* with which I approach such work. . . . It could well be that with the basic objections that you make . . . you are simply touching on my limitations."[14] Bultmann at least attempted a consideration of the tough questions and tried to find adequate language that would be understood by contemporary critics of Christianity. No wonder he felt misunderstood on all sides!

But did he indeed attempt the right thing and fail, or was there a ray of hope in his failure? True, he ended up giving the world a restricted, historical Jesus the Teacher. It may not seem important, half a century later, but that was the Jesus which a positivistic world could tolerate. It would be interesting to investigate how much Jesus would be present in academic discussion today, had Bultmann not jammed his foot in a door that was rapidly closing on Christianity. Also, I am willing to argue that although evangelicals are proud of avoiding his mistakes, they make an awful lot of those mistakes that he rightly criticized. Even if one does not follow the details of his argument, there is much to be learned from it.

It must be admitted that the historical-critical method severely shook the foundation of the Christian faith in the world and the Christian church had no ready answer to such issues. For a long time, the church slept soundly on a set of premeditated doctrines while determining the academic

---

14. Jaspert, *Barth/Bultmann*, p 40.

tone in universities. The shock-waves of doubt hit it hard. Can we blame Bultmann, or anyone else in theological academia, for not giving students comprehensive answers in bite-sized pieces to feed a church which found itself rapidly falling behind what was happening in society? Old answers to old questions are no answers, even if they are right. Even answers expressed in an old language are unhelpful, as they can be misunderstood. It seems to me the problem is much more complex than can be solved by spiritual formation courses, by hammering in doctrine, or by making theological academia 'more practical.'

Therefore, I believe that Bultmann was right when he encouraged a brave, critical, and above all *theoretical* reflection both on new secular-philosophical developments and church-doctrines (even if I tend to disagree with some of his more specific suggestions). Now let me turn from Bultmann to my particular national and academic context. To foreshadow my conclusions, investigating this context will lead me to the same results: what we need is serious *theoretical* work and not an even stronger emphasis on practical issues and spiritual formation in academic studies.

Christian doctrinal mantras of the 'back to orthodox faith' and 'back to practical theology' kind have often been counterproductive. In Croatia, Protestant theology was practically non-existent and there was a dire lack of intellectualism in the churches until only two decades ago – any academic attempts in theology were automatically labelled 'liberal' by church leaders. The task of sound, Bible-believing theological institutions was considered to be 'spiritually formative' and 'practical'. While in some western settings this might have meant being a little less academic; in the Croatian context it naturally translated to ensuring future ministers would be as anti-intellectual as possible, teaching them to copy US models, and instructing them to defend (fight for) 'right' doctrine. Diplomas were awarded to students who could regurgitate learned concepts faultlessly. They were made to feel important by the awarding of academic titles, but remained ineffective and easily manipulated. Is it any wonder that in such a context, evangelicals are often considered to be Americans or American spies, or at least not true Croatians? Add to this the 'missional' method of 'doctrinal war' *against* women, charismatics and Roman Catholics, which is taught in some 'Bible-believing' schools as the only approach, and we are heading for evangelistic disaster in a country seeking answers to its deeply rooted, moral mayhem. Croatia is 85 percent 'proud to be Catholic' in the same manner as it has a small number of evangelicals – charismatics included. The outcome (i.e. the general lack of evangelical witness) should not puzzle us.

Instead, I believe the rhetoric of Evangelical Christianity must be changed and maintain that it is theological academia's business to be theoretical and academic; to be equipped enough in the ways of science and the world to test both doctrine and culture. As early as 1987, David Wenham of Wycliffe Hall in Oxford wrote a booklet on the study of theology as a ministry for Jesus. It was translated and published in Germany by the *Arbeitskreis für evangelikale Theologie* and published by Brockhaus and Brunnen Verlag. In it, he argued for the necessity for continued theological, and indeed, biblical research. Not everything has been said in the two thousand years. Primarily, he thinks that Christian academic work is needed because each period introduces a new set of problems to which responsible biblical answers need to be found.[15] From this perspective, it is the job of theological academia to be theoretical. But we should go even further and notice that the task is not only to train ministers. Rather, we should also expect theological institutions to train people in academic capacities to evaluate and propose solutions for new and even projected circumstances in an ever-changing world, so that the church will not always be trailing behind, as Bultmann complained, but may lead the way. And I believe that it is precisely in this capacity that theological academia primarily assists the church and its mission.

Does this mean that theological institutions are for theoreticians and not for practitioners? Yes and no. On the one hand, if indeed the academic process is defined as the study and re-evaluation of culture trends and doctrines, the study of theology must necessarily be theoretical (i.e. deal with theories and critically reflect on itself). Thus, it should be expected that it will produce theoreticians in the first place. On the other hand, the church also needs practitioners, and while they need a certain level of evaluation skills, their major contribution should be the practical

---

15. David Wenham, *Theologische Forschung als Dienst für Jesus* (Giessen: Brunnen Verlag, 1987), p. 2. Unfortunately, this German pamphlet has no precise information of the original, so I could not access it.

application of theology. Consequently, there must be a place for practical training, even in theological institutions. This is a good place to involve ourselves in some popular Bologna Process discussions in the European setting, as these can help us see what learning outcomes in theological studies should be expected.

The Bologna Process mainly focuses on two 'cycles' in higher education – the 180–240 ECTS Bachelor's degree, and the 120 ECTS Master's degree which can be built on it. It does not recognize what has been a 'fine difference' between two types of higher education in most western countries – university level and vocational college or polytechnic level higher education.[16] Most western countries, including Great Britain and Germany, used to have these two tracks in higher education. The vocational colleges taught future practitioners specializing in a particular area. Academic studies, in which students worked in a field through a faculty within a university setting, were mostly theoretical and research based. While vocational colleges were directed towards practical higher expertise in a certain area, university faculties covered entire disciplines and were geared towards research into and evaluation of these areas.

Higher education institutions, specialized in training of skilled professionals, were a response to the needs of the job market. They are becoming more popular, with the Bologna Process emphasis on the economic viability and employability of graduates. Naturally, there has been a great deal of objection from universities and in particular from humanities and some social sciences faculties, whose usefulness cannot be measured purely in economic terms. On the other hand, society needs thinkers as well as practitioners, so there has been an overlapping of tasks in both universities and vocational colleges. However, it must be recognized that we are looking at two modes of teaching, and it seems to me that both should be maintained within their own scope. Though transfers should be possible, the tracks should be kept clearly apart. As impractical as this distinction is for a process in which mobility and economic viability are the primary criteria, the fine difference must still be preserved. Both practical

---

16. http://www.ond.vlaanderen.be/hogeronderwijs/bologna/documents/MDC/BOLOGNA_DECLARATION1.pdf logged 17 July 2013; http://www.sueddeutsche.de/bildung/entscheidung-uni-oder-fh-der-feine-unterschied-1.1050256 logged 17 July 2013.

know-how and theoretical evaluation of knowledge and practices are important for society. But their methodologies are different.

Theology, more than other academic branches, has attempted to mix the two. I believe the roots of this can be found in the tradition of theology as the *regina scientiae*, the development of universities from within church contexts, and not least in the centuries long union of church and state in many European countries. As academics, we expect to produce skilled practitioners to work in churches, who will also be able to promote church values and doctrine as the outcome of the teaching they have received. This, the favourable outcome of our endeavours, *is* valued by church hierarchies, while often our academic procedures are considered too esoteric and *weltfremd*. On the other hand, interestingly, we have inherited the university system and promoted theoretical and philosophical knowledge for so long that theoretical academics and not the ministers are perceived as 'real' theologians. I believe that the European Bologna Process discussions may help us organize our study expectations more successfully by being aware that there are two tasks and two different methodologies involved in theological studies. But before we turn to these conclusions, it will be helpful to deal with the second problem identified in the introduction: the place and nature of biblical scholarship in Christian academia.

What is Biblical?

So far, we have been concerned mainly with how doctrine and academia are combined, and we have discovered this only happens in a fruitful way if doctrine can be re-evaluated. This has been detected as a problem for theology, as doctrines *per se* are considered unchangeable . But there is another problematic area in theological academia – the relationship between Christian doctrine and the Bible. In practice, most evangelicals claim that their doctrine is strictly biblical and therefore requires undivided and untested endorsement by believers, by clergy and also by the theological academia. The problem for evangelicals in particular emerges from the question – can doctrine be equally or even *more biblical* than the Bible?

Conversely, what happens when it is discovered (or claimed) that a doctrine cannot be upheld by the Bible?

The Cape Town Document answered this by placing the Bible above doctrine, wisely expressing the need to "re-centre the study of the Bible as a core discipline" instead. This is heavily dependent on the evangelical belief that the Bible, being the word of God – has the answers.[17] Are we ready to trust the Bible enough to start re-evaluating doctrine in the light of contemporary rereadings of Scripture? In other words, the document cries out for Biblical theology as the centre of evangelical academia. That, however, has a long, dubious status in theological academia, while doctrinal and philosophical approaches to life and faith are uncontested. The Biblical theology claim is no new claim, and has been discussed at least since Bultmann's demythologizing A-bomb, when he, as it was perceived, abolished the basic doctrines of Christianity by an existential rereading of Scripture which, he hoped, would be more 'understandable' to his positivistic academic friends. The pain of the procedure was unbearable as can be seen in a little booklet addressed to ministers by Fritz Rieneker. *"Erledigt ist die Himmelfahrt Jesu; Erledigt ist die Höllenfahrt Jesu; Erledigt ist der Geister und Dämonenglaube; Die Wunder des NT sind als Wunder erledigt; Erledigt ist die Legende von der Jungfrauengeburt; Der Tod ist nicht der Sünde Sold; Die Erbsünde ist ein untersittlicher Begriff; Jesu Auferstehung ist kein wirkliches Ereignis"* – the content already reads like a scream: "Done is the Ascension of Jesus; Done is Jesus' descension to hell; Done is the belief in spirits and demons; the miracles of the New Testament are done; Done is the legend of the virgin conceptions; Death is not the wage of sin; Original sin is an immoral term; Jesus' Resurrection is no real event!"[18] In the meantime, others have added to this list.

Biblical theology is indeed difficult and feels like walking on a tightrope above Niagara Falls. Philosophical approaches tend to convey much more stability because of their firm lengthy history. But how stable are our doctrines really? As evangelicals who build our theology on the

---

17. Wenham, *Theologische Forschung als Dienst für Jesus,* p. 2.

18. For instance, Fritz Rienecker's, *Stellungnahme zu Bultmanns "Entmythologisierung"* (Wuppertal: Brockhause Verlag, 1951).

Reformation, we too have known their dark side. The language of doctrine can be abused to enslave rather than to save. It can incarcerate people in history without offering answers for the present.

On the other hand, the term *ecclesia semper reformanda* evolved from the Reformation as a present and futurist vision of the church's task to reform itself to be a living example of God's work. The Reformation – regardless of what we might want to believe – liberated the church from the prison of some ancient doctrines by suggesting the rereading of Scripture and asserting its position as the superior source of authority. Martin Luther rediscovered the term 'the righteousness of God' by rereading the text in the Letter to the Romans and realizing a grammatical peculiarity in it. The genitive case could be understood as an *objective genitive,* which 'opened the gates of heaven' for him.[19] The process challenged the church and its doctrine dramatically, but rightfully so, as we all agree. True, the process also exposed the church to being questioned after centuries of undisputed monopoly in orthodoxy and standards. The church was by no means ready for this thoroughgoing re-evaluation, as displayed at various levels by various Reformers during these times. Being evangelicals, we admire the Reformation but believe that in many ways it was not radical enough. At the same time, we are stunned by proposals concerning modern re-evaluations of doctrine and appalled by people like Bultmann, who have tried to perform them.

We should not be. The method of rereading Scripture is the biblical answer to applying Scripture to ever-changing human life. We need not go to rabbinic approaches or look at the interesting layout of the Talmud – where all sorts of conflicting commentaries surround the Word of the Torah. We may not want to look at Jesus who performed such rereadings on a daily basis (Matt 5–7) for, as God, he had the divine right to do so. But I suggest we look at Paul's redefinition of core Jewish doctrines. The role of the Law in salvation history, or Abraham and Adam in the Letter to the Romans, are amazing examples of biblical theology's re-evaluation of

---

19. G. Theissen, "Protestantische Exegese. Plädoyer für einen neuen vierfachen Schriftsinn", 1; http://www.google.si/search?q=G.+Theissen,+%27Protestantische+Exege se.+Pl%C3%A4doyer+&ie=utf-8&oe=utf-8&rls=org.mozilla:hr:official&client=firefox-a&gws_rd=cr last accessed 23 August 2013.

doctrines. The Law gives way to Christ as a means of salvation; Abraham becomes the father of the Gentiles, and Adam the father of the Jews who do not accept Christ. As drastic as Paul's redefinitions are, they cannot be viewed as new revelations to Paul. Rather, Paul's solutions are dependent on the revealed and living Word of God.[20] Paul's redefinitions are worthwhile examples because they come down hard on traditions (even basic, identity-forming traditions) but never lose sight of Scripture. The 'new' doctrines are thus not 'new revelation' (Gal 1:8) but are deeply rooted in the revealed Word of God. Such 'new' doctrines become, as Luther put it, 'a door to paradise' for many; in Paul's case, a door for the salvation of Gentiles. As theologians, we are not Paul the apostle, and our redefinitions will not become Scripture, but Paul shows us how redefinitions of doctrine can support God's mission in the world in an amazing way.

Some Concluding Propositions

In conclusion, I would like to propose some practical steps for the church and theological academia concerning the spiritual formation of ministers.

First, the church and academia can only assist processes of growth and formation which are initiated and carried out by the Holy Spirit. Both the academic process and dependence on the Spirit of God suggest that the whole educational and academic process is shaky and cannot, or probably should not, always be controlled. Thus, it is not necessarily the fault of theological academia if some new theologians are not useful to the church. It may even be in certain cases that the church, rather than the theologians, needs to change. Adequate doctrine is a functional means for evangelism and for primary instruction in faith, like a stake to which a young tree is bound to prevent it from breaking and ensure it grows up straight. But Christians must grow beyond the first condensed, abbreviated instructions and start living and bringing forth the fruit of the Spirit. Just as a tree can never bear fruit if it is constantly trimmed back to fit the supporting stake,

---

20. I have shown these processes in *Paul's Territoriality and Missionary Strategy.* Tübingen: Mohr/Siebeck, 2009 and in "Adam naš otac" forthcoming in Obnovljeni život 3 (2013).

Christians and theologians in particular must be allowed to grow beyond the expected. The Bible should be considered richer than our doctrine. We must expect our students to grow in directions we have never thought of and we must allow them to minister to a world which is theirs and may no longer be ours.

Second, I commend *The Cape Town Commitment's* endorsement of (theological) education as an intrinsically missional activity of the church. The church, at least in our part of the world, has been short-sighted for too long, emphasizing *only* evangelism (and then only 'preaching the Word') as the sole, intrinsically missional activity of the church. Although the document does not state it specifically, it presupposes an all-round theological education which would include practical and theoretical courses. Theological academia's task would be so much easier if all aspects of the theological task were appreciated by the church.

Thirdly, within such contexts, all scholarship should be welcome, bearing in mind the finality of both scholarship and the church's conceptions. We may want to separate the tasks of theological instruction to make it easier for students: in other words to train practitioners in one track and theological academics in a different track, but allow for transfers. Not everybody displays pastoral capacities, and not everybody can be expected to evaluate traditions theoretically and think theologically. But we need to understand that both types of theologians are in the ministry of the church. Generally, the church may prefer ministers, as academics tend to bring unsettling thoughts and upset routines. Also, let us face it – academics rarely make good practitioners, but practitioners too should beware of making academic judgments (for instance determining who is too liberal, or what is biblical). Each should develop their own area but they all should be willing to investigate points of encounter. In this the Bologna Process 'life-long learning' concept must be considered mandatory. Life-long learning among professionals provides a point of encounter between theological academia and church leaders. It gives a good perspective on the practice of faith in life to the theoreticians, while the practitioners develop the ability to recognize and implement necessary changes in their approaches.

We must bear in mind that not everything which surfaces in academic discourse needs to be presented to the churches. But that does not automatically mean that the stuff of academic discussion is unspiritual or impractical. There are vital steps in thought processes that need to be taken, language barriers crossed and new terminologies invented to fit the needs of an ever-changing world. No academic can see *all* the implications and threats and paradigm shifts at the beginning of an idea or evaluation. The 'Bultmanns' of our day cannot be prevented from appearing in academia (and probably they should not). They too have their place. As academics, we must know how to admit in humility that our knowledge is partial and sometimes distorted. And so must the church.

Special thanks to Janet Berković for proofreading this article.

Bibliography

Birdsall, D and L. Brown, eds. *The Cape Town Commitment.* http://www.lausanne.org/en/documents/ctcommitment.html#p2–6

Bowers, P. *Evangelical Theological Education: An International Agenda.* Springwood: International Council of Accrediting Agencies, 1994.

Bultmann, R. *Existence & Faith: Shorter Writings of Rudolf Bultmann.* New York: Meridian Books, 1960.

Hardy, S. A. *Excellence in Theological Education: Effective Training for Church Leaders.* S. Hardy, 2006.

Hunt, G. L. *Ten Makers of Modern Protestant Thought.* New York: Association Press, 1958.

Holmes, A. F. *Building the Christian Academy.* Grand Rapids: Eerdmans, 2001.

Hughes, P. E.. *Creative Minds in Contemporary Theology.* Grand Rapids: Eerdmans, 1969.

Jaspers, K. and R. Bultmann. *Myth and Christianity: An Inquiry into the Possibility of Religion Without Myth.* New York: Noonday Press, 1958.

Jaspert, Bernd, ed. *Karl Barth – Rudolf Bultmann: Letters 1922–1966.* Edinburgh: T & T Clark, 1982.

Magda, K. "Adam, naš otac: Kako je apostol Pavao 'popravio' tradicije, a potvrdio Pisma" in *Obnovljeni život* (2013), forthcoming.

———. *Paul's Territoriality and Mission Strategy.* Tübingen: Mohr-Siebeck, 2009.

Macquarrie, John. "Philosophy and Theology in Bultmann's Thought" in Charles W. Kegley, ed. *The Theology of Rudolf Bultmann*, New York: Harper & Row, 1966.

Rienecker, Fritz. *Stellungnahme zu Bultmanns 'Entmythologisierung'*. Wuppertal: Brockhaus Verlag, 1951.

Theissen, G. "Protestantische Exegese: Plädoyer für einen neuen vierfachen Schriftsinn", Paper at Waldenserfakultät, Rome, March 3, 2005. http://www.google.si/search?q=G.+Theissen,+%27Protestantische+Exegese.+Pl%C3%A4doyer+&ie=utf-8&oe=utf-8&rls=org.mozilla:hr:official&client=firefox-a&gws_rd=cr

Thielicke, Helmut. *Zu Gast auf einem schönen Stern*. 6th ed. Hamburg: Hoffmann und Campe, 1986.

Wenham, David. *Theologische Forschung als Dienst für Jesus*. Gießen: Brunnen Verlag, 1987.

CHAPTER 3

From Knowledge to Understanding: Teaching Systematic Theology after Modernity

Dóra Bernhardt

What shapes theological education? There are, of course, many different answers to this very general question. For example, David Kelsey in his fine book, *To Understand God Truly: What's Theological About a Theological School?*[1], proposes that what makes a theological school 'theological' is being "a group of persons whose overarching end is to understand God more truly" and, based on this definition, introduces the reader to different answers given to the question, "How we can understand God?" across the ages. He claims "the diversity of ways in which the Christian thing is construed makes the world of theological schools irreducibly pluralistic. . . . Different construals bring with them significantly different notions of what it would be to 'understand' God truly."[2] Thus, *sapientia* (contemplation), *scientia* (discursive reasoning), *unitio* (the affections) and *praxis* (action) are some of the ways that different branches or groups of the church in different cultural-historical periods understood both what Kelsey calls 'the Christian thing' and consequently the way of truly understanding God. Kelsey's four main types of understanding to some extent correspond to

---

1. David H. Kelsey, *To Understand God Truly: What's Theological About a Theological School?* (Louisville, Kentucky: Westminster/John Knox Press, 1992) republished in 2011 as *Between Athens and Berlin: The Theological Education Debate.*
2. Ibid., p. 34.

the emphases of particular denominational or theological traditions: the affections, for example, play a significant role in the Pentecostal approach to understanding God, while *praxis* or action is the most important element of a true knowledge of God for liberation theologies. *Sapientia*, which, by way of contemplation, focuses on the beatific vision of the unchanging God, has been definitive in Eastern Orthodoxy. Understanding God through *scientia*, Kelsey notes, was influential in both late-Western medieval and modern theological schooling and "continues to shape many North American theological schools historically rooted in certain Roman Catholic communities . . . and schools rooted in the Reformed tradition."[3]

Of course, Kelsey himself is clear about the fact that church traditions are only one factor when trying to establish how a particular theological school construes the goal of understanding God. Other factors can be just as influential, for example, historical, social and cultural considerations. In the following I want to argue that in the present context of western Protestant and evangelical education, primarily *scientia*-oriented theological schools, our 'postmodern' cultural and scientific milieu moves us in the same direction that Kelsey imagines for theological schools, namely towards a plurality of approaches in theological education. Second, I want to suggest concrete ways of doing so.

After Modernity

From a scientific point of view education, and thus theological education, is closely related to two areas of enquiry: epistemology and anthropology. We want to impart knowledge, and the way we do this is, to a large extent, determined by what we think about who we are, and thus of how we learn. Today it is a truism to assert that what we call 'modernity' brought with it radically new ways of thinking about both of these. To put it very simply, and thus necessarily superficially, from the late Middle Ages onwards, knowledge came to be regarded as the making of 'objectively' true statements about the world around us and thus imposing 'a mental order

---

3. Ibid., p. 41.

on the chaos that surrounds us.'[4] Accordingly, we as humans came to be regarded as *homo sapiens*, 'knowing man', or, based on Descrates' "Cogito, ergo sum," dictum – "thinking things" – for whom reason as discursive rationality and history as progress formed the basis of a secure meta-narrative. At the same time, "these old verities of modernity demanded for their pure observance a harsh and pristine separation of thought from feeling, form from content, and most devastatingly, theory from practice."[5] In this milieu, the task of education was increasingly seen to somehow plant the content of this mental order in students' minds – although, of course, exceptions to the rule were always around.

Many changes have happened in the last 60 or 70 years, however. After Auschwitz, old certainties began to be questioned and then died as "in the maelstrom of the twentieth century [the above mentioned] divisions of existence have come to be seen as dangerously naïve, repressive of wholeness, and hopelessly flatfooted."[6] Both epistemology and anthropology have been affected by the so-called postmodern turn, with which by now we are all too familiar (so I will not spend time attempting to define or describe this historically and theoretically complex phenomenon). Suffice it to say that the changes in our view, after modernity, of what knowledge is about as well as who we are as humans have many different aspects and can be delineated in many ways. One aspect has to do with the emphasis shifting from the cognitive, that is, our thinking, our minds, to the non-cognitive, that is, to the role that our feelings or affections, our imagination and desires as well as our bodies play in both who we are and how we know the world around us. Several hundred books have been written about different aspects of 'The Body' and 'Desire' by both Christian and 'postmodern' thinkers. Some educators have worded this idea in terms of a juxtaposition of knowledge and understanding. "To understand is 'to comprehend', and to comprehend is 'to take in' or embrace" – says

---

4. Parker Palmer, *To Know as We Are Known* (San Francisco: Harper San Francisco, 1993) p. 3.
5. Mark A. McIntosh, *Mystical Theology* (Malde, Massachutes/Oxford, UK: Blackwell Publishers, 1998), p. 4.
6. Ibid.

professor Y. K. Ip in the e-journal *Successful Learning*,[7] and his view seems to echo Albert Einstein, according to whom "Any fool can know. The point is to understand." Canadian philosopher Charles Taylor, too, has drawn attention to the difference between knowledge as represented by ideas and theory and what he – following Martin Heidegger – terms 'understanding.' Like Heidegger's '*Verstehen*', which is an "inarticulate understanding of our whole situation" and constitutes the background of our knowledge (*Wissen*),[8] Taylor's 'understanding' has to do with seeing the *meaning* of things and is thus, sooner or later, always expressed in practice. At the same time, understanding is not dialectically opposed to knowledge; "what's understood in the practice can be somewhat articulated in theory or doctrine."[9]

Another important aspect of Taylor's 'understanding' which differentiates it from 'knowledge' clarifies the anthropology behind the two. Smith puts it in the following way: "Taylor intuits that what we 'think about' is just the tip of the iceberg and cannot fully or even adequately account for how and why we make our way in the world. There's something else and something more rumbling beneath the cognitive that drives much of our action and behaviour."[10] This 'something more', rumbling beneath, has been described by psychology as our pre-cognitive subconscious, with its many different facets and origins; but, I want to argue, this anthropology is also in line with pre-modern thought and with how the Bible sees us humans: not as primarily thinking things, but as 'body-persons', who are, for the most part, 'desiring, imaginative, noncognitive animals'[11] with an openness toward that which transcends us. At the same time, there is no doubt that we are also defined by our social and cultural environment. This is what Taylor calls the 'social imaginary', which is "often not expressed in theoretical terms, but is carried in images, stories, and legends . . . [and is]

---

7. http://www.cdtl.nus.edu.sg/success/sl20.htm

8. Quoted in James K. A. Smith, *Desiring the Kingdom: Worship, Worldview, and Cultural Formation* (Grand Rapids: Baker Academic, 2009) p. 66.

9. Ibid., p. 68.

10. Ibid., p. 65.

11. Ibid., p. 56.

shared by large groups of people [and] makes possible common practices and a widely shared sense of legitimacy."[12]

Systematic Theology after Modernity

If all of this is true to the way things are and to how we as humans function, how does this affect theological education? Of course, theological education itself is a wide field where the way we approach and teach Biblical studies will no doubt differ from how we teach, say, counselling.[13] In the following I will focus mainly on systematic theology; partly because that is where my interests lie, but also because, by definition, systematic/dogmatic theology is the discipline most prone to a 'modernist', discursive reason-based approach.

I want to propose four possible ways of going beyond the modern emphasis on reason and cognition, and incorporating the old/new emphasis that takes seriously our desires and imagination as well as the bodily rootedness of our humanity in the context of our Western Protestant/ evangelical academic environment.[14] These are 1) a renewed emphasis on spirituality as both an academic discipline and praxis; 2) the use of the arts in teaching theology; 3) the primary role of practices as opposed to worldview in our academic approach; and 4) intercultural theology as a way of being challenged by non-Western ways of doing theology. Given the limits of this paper, my proposal will necessarily be more of an invitation to an exchange of ideas for the sake of shared understanding than a well-developed, detailed suggestion. The four concrete suggestions thus remain

---

12. Charles Taylor, *Modern Social Imaginaries* (Durham, NC: Duke University Press, 2004), p. 23.

13. The question whether particular areas of theological enquiry, such as biblical studies, systematic theology, pastoral theology, etc. should be so clearly isolated or rather somehow integrated is itself a matter of contention, but I do not see any realistic hope of change in the near future, so I will here assume that most theological schools will continue to offer separate courses in these fields.

14. The original version of this paper was given in a Central European context. However, I think that even though Central-Eastern Europe is in some ways still less 'Western' than our West European neighbours, the main thrust of our theological education can be characterized as 'Western'.

on the general level, with just one or two examples, and I will not offer any curricula or even fully worked-out lesson plans. I take full responsibility for this though, as I am convinced that a discussion of general directions is where any change must start.

1) Spirituality

Even though spiritual formation, sometimes called 'discipleship', has always been an important focus of evangelical theological schools (though not always so in mainline Protestant denominational seminaries), traditional western spirituality as part of an academic curriculum has only recently been rediscovered in English-speaking countries. This change has been partly caused by the influence of writers such as Thomas Merton and Henri Nouwen, and partly by the recent postmodern interest in spirituality. The Pentecostal/charismatic movements of the twentieth century have also redirected attention to the importance of spiritual formation, but in many Protestant theological schools, at least in my experience, spirituality as an academic discipline is still often regarded 'a Catholic thing'.

In theory, every theologian would affirm Thomas Merton's words that "we must not separate intellectual study of divine revealed truth and contemplative experience of that truth as if they could never have anything to do with one another. . . . This fallacious division perhaps explains much that is actually lacking both in theology and spirituality. But the two belong together. Unless they are united, there is no fervour, no life and no spiritual value in theology."[15]

How this can be done is, of course, a much more complex issue, and one that also presents its difficulties. After all, one reason why emotions and desires have not been part of (formal) theological education is that they seem to be so 'subjective', so elusive and contingent. As Anne Hunt put it, commenting on the inclusion of this area in theological education, "perhaps along with this positive recognition is the needed realization that there are some things that simply cannot be taught or assessed as part of a seminary curriculum. . . . Giving grades for spiritual disciplines is like

---

15. Thomas Merton, *Seeds of Contemplation*, Anthony Clarke Books, 1972, 197–198. Quoted in McIntosh, *Mystical Theology*, p. 10.

trying to describe the beauty of a painting or explain a Beethoven sonata's appeal to the heart, and then giving it a letter grade."[16] Clearly there are different ways of approaching and teaching Christian spirituality: from biblical, historical, denominational, missiological, spiritual disciplines, etc., perspective, and the problem of evaluation as addressed by Hunt above is one of the issues that, unfortunately, cannot be discussed in the framework of this paper. The fact, however, that several theological schools now have courses in Christian spirituality is a sign that it might, after modernity, be possible to return to the "more classical notion of mind [which] refers to the desire of our whole being for deep understanding and relationship with all that is intelligible,"[17] including individual doctrines, I would add.

2) The Arts

After modernity, we ascertained above, we do not trust our minds to tell us the truth any more. We have rediscovered our bodies, our emotions, our imagination – and what would be a better vehicle for these than the arts. The relationship between the arts and theology is, of course, as old as that between theology and spirituality (which were not even two different things, to begin with) and thousands of books and articles have been written about this relationship. There are many professors of theology – as there are many people in general – for whom the arts are an important part of life, and who use the arts to illustrate their teaching of theology, because they realize that in theology "the arts can play one of their most crucial roles, for their immense *integrative* power is unquestionable: their ability to reunite the intellect with the other facets of our makeup – our bodies, wills, emotional life, and so on."[18]

The arts can offer even more than illustration. They analogically express something of the truth of God and the world that cannot always be expressed conceptually, and can thus contribute to a true understanding of God. In

16. Anne Hunt, "'To live is to change; to be perfect is to have changed often': Challenges, imperatives and opportunities for theology in the 21st century." *Australian eJournal of Theology 18.2 (August 2011)* 117.

17. McIntosh, p. 11.

18. Jeremy Begbie, ed. *Sounding the Depths: Theology Through the Arts* (London: SCM Press, 2002) p. 7.

the words of Tom Wright, a renowned professor of New Testament, "If all theology, all sermons, had to be set to music, our teaching and preaching would not only be more mellifluous; it might also approximate more closely to God's truth, the truth revealed in and as the Word made flesh, crucified and risen."[19] How to apply this insight in theological education, especially in teaching systematic theology, is a challenge that is both difficult and exhilarating and which, again, has been explored by many scholars and educators in the context of different forms of art. In the above-mentioned book, edited by Begbie, music is the main vehicle of a "performance of theology through the arts" which goes beyond using music only as a means of worship but does justice to the power of music to express truth in a way that words are not able to. In the twenty-first century, film has become another art form, which is often used by teachers as a means of conveying theological truth.[20]

Once again, within the limits of this paper this topic can only be treated superficially, as one of the special ways of teaching (systematic) theology in an age where we put more leverage on the imagination and other non-cognitive forms of understanding theological truth, and thus leave it to the reader to evaluate concrete ways of putting this into practice.

3) Practices

We saw above that according to Charles Taylor, common pratices are an important form of the 'social imaginary', the set of values, symbols, laws, etc., that shape who we are and how we behave at a non- or pre-cognitive level. James K. A. Smith employs two examples to illustrate the idea of this level of consciousness which I think are helpful. One is Eugene Peterson's translation in the *Message* of the word *kardia* (heart) as *gut*, "which captures both a sense of this bowel-level centre of gravity of our identity, as well as the grittiness of its embodiment."[21] Smith argues that the way we make our

---

19. N. T. Wright, "Resurrection: From Theology to Music and Back Again" in Begbie, ibid., pp. 210–211.
20. Cf., for example, Christopher K. Richardson, "Special Pathos: The Roles of Art in Theological Education," *Journal of Adult Theological Education*. Dec 2009, Vol. 6, Issue 2, pp. 130–140.
21. Smith, p. 57.

way around in the world is less by our mind or intellect than our feeling, our imagination; that rather than our worldview, it is our habit or *habitus* that will ultimately decide the way we lead our lives. Habits, Smith argues, constitute our 'second nature', and even though they can be learned, "they can become so intricately woven into the fibre of our being that they function *as if* they were our biological nature."[22] In turn, it is bodily practices and rituals that inscribe habits and dispositions in us. The example Smith uses here is that of finding a letter on the keyboard of our computer: if someone asked us what the letter next to the 'F' is, we probably would not be able to immediately tell them; it is our *fingers* rather than our mind that possesses this knowledge. That is what bodily practices are like, he insists: "How did your hands get to 'know' this? Through rituals, routines, and exercises that trained your adaptive unconscious. These exercises put your body through the motions over and over again until this know-how became lodged in a part of your brain that you don't often call to mind."[23] Importantly, Smith argues, whether we recognize it or not, we take part in the secular practices or 'rituals' of our age and society, whether these be checking our Facebook profile first thing in the morning, going to the shopping mall, or the 'liturgies of the university' that take place not only in the classroom or lab but at Freshers' Week, at graduation, etc.[24]

What has all this got to do with teaching systematic theology, however? If the above is right, our knowledge of God also exists on more than the level of our minds; furthermore, if our secular practices and rituals form us at a pre-cognitive level, we have to be aware of the possibility of *mis*-formation and *counter*-formation, as Smith says.[25] The only way to let God's truth (doctrines) get to the non-cognitive levels of our minds and to counter secular practices will then be through 'faith' practices. This is nothing new, of course: on the individual level, spiritual disciplines are one example of the bodily practices that support and deepen a person's spiritual life.[26] On the level of the community of the church, however, it is the

---

22. Ibid., p. 56.
23. Ibid., p. 59.
24. See Ibid., pp. 112–121.
25. Ibid., pp. 75–88.
26. See e.g. Adele Ahlberg Calhoun, *Spiritual Disciplines Handbook: Practices that*

liturgy with all its symbolism that builds just on this experience. Singing God's praises, confessing our sins, receiving absolution, taking communion as a sign of Jesus' having given himself for us, etc., are all *bodily* practices that can, and often do, help us understand God's truth at a level that goes deeper than our conscious minds. Of course, there is a psychology to these practices as well: the more regularly we engage in them, the more effective they are, and vice versa. Monastic communities know this well, as is attested in the daily office and other, more 'worldy' practices of these local 'theological communities'.

But how can practices be incorporated into teaching theology? Seminaries have to be creative here, I think, building both on tradition and on new ideas. Most theological schools incorporate some form of liturgical practice into their academic life: daily or weekly services/devotions, prayer or community groups, sometimes meals together, are meant to provide the 'practical' (in all meanings of the word) underlining of the theology learned in classes. These do not always get connected in students' minds and hearts, however. They are tested or examined on the *doctrine*, for example of the atonement, but there is no evaluation of their *practice* of the Eucharist – how could there be? One way to bring the two closer together could be connecting the doctrine and the practice more closely in time and space by, for example, taking communion when studying the death and resurrection of Jesus or the Eucharist, or talking honestly about one's personal experience of confession and absolution in the liturgy when studying the atonement. Thankfully, there are more and more examples of groups of students leaving the safe haven of the seminary and sharing life – to some extent – with the homeless, the physically or mentally challenged, children, etc., all of which are *practices* of the incarnation. It is important, though, that practices are not one-off events, but have to be done repeatedly in order for them to 'train the adaptive unconscious'. Reflecting on these practices together or individually can also be an important part of the learning process, although the danger of 'rationalizing' has to be kept in mind.

Transform Us (Downers Grove, Illinois: IVP, 2005).

4) Intercultural Theology

One of the marks of 'modernity' as defined above is that it emerged in Europe and is thus closely connected to western (including, besides Europe, other European-based societies) ways of thinking. Thus, after modernity, one of the significant intellectual moves – at least in theory – has been 'decolonization' and, parallel with it, 'de-westernization'. As the last approach to teaching theology after modernity, I would like to claim that 'intercultural theology' (or 'world Christianity' as it is sometimes called), defined as "a contemporary approach to theology, one that pays particular attention to the culture in which theology is set"[27] and focuses mainly on non-western forms of Christianity, can provide helpful examples of doing (systematic) theology after modernity.

There are many aspects of non-western theologies that could be and have been analyzed. In the context of the present paper, however, I would like to focus on the fact that due to their socio-economic and cultural 'situatedness', non-western theologies have *always* – though in different cultures in different ways – been more attentive to the *praxis* of the Christian faith; that is, western modernity's separation of theory from praxis, of dogma from life, has not been a problem that had to wait for the arrival of post-modernity to be addressed. This is how Kosuke Koyama expressed this attitude in his oft-quoted book *Waterbuffalo Theology*: "I decided to subordinate great theological thoughts, like those of Thomas Aquinas and Karl Barth, to the intellectual and spiritual needs of the farmers. I decided that the greatness of theological works is to be judged by the extent and quality of the service they can render to the farmers to whom I am sent. I also decided that I have not really understood *Summa Theologiae* or *Church Dogmatics* until I am able to use them for the benefit of the farmers."[28]

Similarly, Andrew Wildsmith in his paper "Contextualizing the Structure of Systematic Theology in Africa"[29] recommends a "radical

---

27. Mark J. Cartledge and David Cheetham, eds. *Intercultural Theology: Approaches and Themes* (London: SCM Press, 2011), p. 1.

28. Kosuke Koyama, *Waterbuffalo Theology* (Maryknoll, New York: Orbis Books, 1974), p. ix.

29. Andrew Wildsmith, "Contextualizing the Structure of Systematic Theology in Africa" in *Evangelical Review of Theology*, Apr 2011, Vol. 35 Issue 2, pp 122–139.

departure from traditional western categories for systematic theology" by reintegrating the traditional disciplines and contextualizing the structure of (systematic) theology so as to "help students to connect more closely important theological concepts with real ministry needs."[30] This is a very similar concern to that of Koyama. One could go on to study Asian, South American or aboriginal theologies and discern approaches to systematic theology that sound very unusual for a western mind. However, much of what non-western theologians and theologies emphasize rhyme with the pre- and post-modern emphasis we mentioned at the beginning of this paper: less reliance on reason and the cognitive and more on the pre-cognitive, the imagination and bodily practices/habits and symbols, thus a more integrated approach between theory and praxis and action.

This commitment was expressed at a conference in Dar-es-Salaam in the following way: "We reject as irrelevant an academic type of theology that is divorced from action. We are prepared for a radical break in epistemology which makes commitment the first act of theology and engages in critical reflection on the praxis of the reality of the Third World."[31] In Central Europe we are closer to the First than to the Third World in terms of culture, but I am convinced that this approach could nonetheless fruitfully renew – or at least refresh – the teaching of systematic theology in our part of the world, too. For example, we could ask, following Koyama, how the theology of Luther, Barth, etc., could be used for the benefit of the Hungarian people in 2013, or, with Wildsmith, what the ministry needs of a congregation in 2013 are and how the structure of our curriculum of systematic theology could better serve those.

Conclusion

My aim in this paper was not to say the last word on the topic of teaching (systematic) theology after modernity. If anything, postmodernity teaches

---

30. Ibid., p. 123.

31. Quoted in Kwame Bediako, *Christianity in Africa: The Renewal of a Non-Western Religion* (Edinburgh / Maryknoll: Edinburgh University Press / Orbis Books, 1995) p. 160.

us that there *is* no one right way of doing things; and David Kelsey seems to agree when suggesting that a plurality of approaches might also be the way forward in theological education. I think it has become clear from what was said so far that I agree with the need for theological education, especially the teaching of systematic theology, to make 'understanding' rather than 'knowledge' its goal. What I hope to have done in this paper is to suggest some ways of doing this, while realizing that, given the pressures of academic excellence, this is not an easy task. It is the task of the community of scholars to find the way forward, and I hope to have contributed something to that end.

Bibliography

Bediako, Kwame. *Christianity in Africa: The Renewal of a Non-Western Religion.* Edinburgh / Maryknoll: Edinburgh University Press / Orbis Books, 1995.

Begbie, Jeremy, ed. *Sounding the Depths: Theology Through the Arts.* London: SCM Press, 2002.

Calhoun, Adele Ahlberg. *Spiritual Disciplines Handbook: Practices that Transform Us.* Downers Grove, Illinois: IVP, 2005.

Cartledge, Mark J. and David Cheetham, eds. *Intercultural Theology: Approaches and Themes.* London: SCM Press, 2011.

Hunt, Anne. "'To live is to change; to be perfect is to have changed often': Challenges, imperatives and opportunities for theology in the 21st century", *Australian eJournal of Theology,* 18.2, (August 2011): 117.

Ip, Y. K. "Knowing is Not the Same as Understanding: What is Understanding?" Centre for Development of Teaching and Learning (CDTL). Available through http://www.cdtl.nus.edu.sg/success/sl20.htm

Kelsey, David H. *To Understand God Truly: What's Theological About a Theological School?* Louisville, Kentucky: Westminster/John Knox Press, 1992. republished in 2011 as *Between Athens and Berlin: The Theological Education Debate.*

Koyama, Kosuke. *Waterbuffalo Theology.* Maryknoll, New York: Orbis Books, 1974.

McIntosh, Mark A. *Mystical Theology.* Malde, Massachutes/Oxford, UK: Blackwell Publishers, 1998.

Merton, Thomas. *Seeds of Contemplation.* New York: New Directions, 1972.

Palmer, Parker. *To Know as We Are Known.* San Francisco: Harper San Francisco, 1993.

Richardson, Christopher K. "Special Pathos: The Roles of Art in Theological Education," *Journal of Adult Theological Education*, Vol. 6, Issue 2, (Dec 2009): 130–140.

Smith, James K. A. *Desiring the Kingdom: Worship, Worldview, and Cultural Formation.* Grand Rapids: Baker Academic, 2009.

Taylor, Charles. *Modern Social Imaginaries.* Durham, NC: Duke University Press, 2004.

Wright, N. T. "Resurrection: From Theology to Music and Back Again" in Begbie, J., ed. *Sounding the Depths: Theology Through the Arts.* London: SCM Press, 2002, pp. 210–211.

Wildsmith, Andrew. "Contextualizing the Structure of Systematic Theology in Africa" in *Evangelical Review of Theology*, Vol. 35, Issue 2, (Apr 2011): 122–139.

CHAPTER 4

Developing Missional Leaders in the Reformed Church in Hungary: Missional Leadership in the City

András Lovas

"It has been a long time since I experienced such an intensive spiritual and intellectual transformation." This is a beautiful sentence for a pastor's ears. To see people being transformed and refreshed by the power of the gospel is the pastor's passion. However, this sentence was not born on a church retreat, but after an academic theology course. Now, theological training seldom provokes such enthusiastic statements about personal transformation. This paper is about how to integrate academic, spiritual, and missiological dimensions in a theology course so that it would inspire such sentences.

In the following I reflect on my experience of teaching elective courses in urban mission for students of theology at Karoli Gaspar University. (Some of these courses comprised a part of my Doctor of Ministry project by the title above.)[1] The paper starts with the church context in which the idea of missional leadership is introduced. This concept, based on the work of Lesslie Newbigin and developed by the *Gospel and Our Culture Network*, is contrasted with what we call the maintenance and pragmatic models of church leadership. Second, I outline the content and method of

---

1. The course *Urban Mission on the Housing Estate* was taught in 2005 and 2007. I also led another course in 2011 titled *Church Planting in Urban Context*. This course built on similar missiological foundations and utilized similar methods as the previous ones.

the courses. Introducing ministry site experiences throughout the courses seemed to be significant for the transformation of the students' missional vision and spirituality. Personal reflection encouraged students to face the questions of their calling. Finally, as being primarily a local church pastor, I try to summarize relevant issues for theological education in our context.

The Problem to be Addressed: What Kind of Leadership?

In my dissertation I raised the question of the apparent weakness and reluctance of the Hungarian Reformed Church to plant urban churches and develop innovative ministries on the housing estates of Hungary. It is argued that a new paradigm of pastoral leadership is required in this situation, one I identified as missional leadership. The courses addressed that need to nurture and develop pastors as missional leaders.

The Crisis of the Mission of the Church

The churches of the Central and Eastern European region lived in isolation from the mainstream society under the Communist dictatorship between 1948–1990. In Hungary the Hungarian Reformed Church (HRC), along with a number of other churches, received a legal status of freedom in 1990 and found itself in a new situation. After many years of restriction and lack of freedom, unexpected doors opened. But the churches had to realize that they were not prepared for freedom among these new opportunities. This conclusion is reached by István Bogárdi Szabó, who analyzed four written evaluations, all of which attempted to evaluate the life and mission of the HRC ten years after the democratic changes.[2] He points out that all four authors – having the mission of the church as one of their main evaluative principles – express their criticism related to the issue of mission. The HRC is assessed by the presence or the absence of mission activities, by the strengths

---

2. István Bogárdi Szabó, "Az MRE elmúlt tíz évének írásos értékelései" (The Written Evaluations of the Past 10 years of the Reformed Church in Hungary), *THÉMA* 3. No. 1 (2001), p. 14–27.

or weaknesses demonstrated in her mission.[3] One evaluation underlines the lack of missional vision, a comprehensive concept and strategy, and states that the evangelization of society and the inner evangelization of the church did not happen.[4] Another evaluation points to the visible results of building projects, establishing a school system, but sadly voices that the morals further decreased in Hungary.[5] A third assessment makes the criticism that the HRC seems to replace mission with large demonstrations and political ideology.[6] All these papers point to the crisis of mission and the weakness the HRC is experiencing. That crisis leads to the issue of pastoral leadership since the primary mission frontier is that of the local congregation, the gathered community of those who profess Jesus Christ as Lord. The question is what the task of pastoral leadership is in the context of mission crisis. There can be three basic responses to this question.

Leadership: Maintenance, Pragmatic or Missional?

One response with which a number of pastors and other church leaders identified themselves after the democratic changes is the maintenance model, which builds on the church's Christendom experience. The idea is to turn towards the past and try to continue the life of the church where it was forcefully disrupted in 1948. The church of the Christendom assumes a strong relationship between state and church, presupposes a privileged position of the church in the society, and builds the church's life and mission on the assumption that all members of (the Christian) society belong to the church. The model of Christendom, however, as promising and attractive as it is, cannot help. Sándor Fazakas, in his doctoral dissertation on the ecclesiology of the HRC after World War II, reviews the analysis of Eberhard Stammler. Stammler considers the Central-Eastern European churches' attempt to integrate into the changed social context a restoration of the *people's church* – or Christendom church – model. Stammler names three aspects of this integration: the introduction of Christian religious

---

3. Ibid., p. 25.
4. Ibid., p. 18–19.
5. Ibid., p. 21.
6. Ibid., p. 23.

education classes in schools, military chaplaincy, and the church tax system
(well-known in Western Europe). He believes that the western model is
attractive, especially as one looks at the affluence and the influence of
western churches, but at the same time these developments might result in
missing the opportunity of restructuring the church on a biblical-reformed
basis.[7]

In the last twenty or more years the ministry of the HRC, for the most
part, has been imagined in a Christendom model. It is demonstrated by the
frequently asked question of how to invite those 1.6 million people into
the Reformed churches who professed themselves 'Reformed' according to
the national census in 2001.[8] The main characteristic of this approach is
that it takes the denominational division, as well as the nominal Christian
consciousness, for granted. Mission is geared towards them presupposing
that they are Reformed, and, as a consequence, still understand and
somewhat honour the Reformed heritage and doctrines. At the same time,
emphasizing that its mission is towards those who have been baptized
as Reformed, the HRC seems to ignore those who professed themselves
Roman Catholic or gave any other responses.[9] According to this logic, since
the Reformed belong to the church, HRC pastors can do mission work in

---

7. Sándor Fazakas, Új *egyház felé? A második világháború utáni református egyházi*
megújulás ekkléziológiai konzekvenciái ("Towards a new church?" The Ecclesiological
Consequences of the Reformed Church Renewal after the Second World War) (Debrecen:
Debreceni Református Kollégium, 2000), p. 97. Though using the term *Western example*
referring to Western European churches, Fazakas particularly mentions only two
countries, Germany and Switzerland. It should be noted that the framework of church-
state relationship differs from country to country.

8. The results of the 2011 census became public recently. They demonstrated a
definite decrease in the number of those who identified themselves as 'Reformed'. The
interpretation of the data is controversial due to the different questions at the 2001 and
2011 censuses.

9. The weakness of this thinking is clearly demonstrated by the following figures.
In Budapest's eleventh district, where the Gazdagrét Reformed Church is situated,
144,441 people took part in the census. There are 70,057 Roman and Greek Catholic,
17,327 Reformed, 4,088 Lutheran, 656 Israelite, and 2,241 claimed to belong to other
denominations. The number of those who do not belong to any church is 26,076, while
21,956 refused to respond. Even if one supposes that the 70,057 Roman Catholics are
actively practicing their religion (which is far from the truth), still there are almost three
times as many people who do not respond or do not belong to any church than those
who professed themselves Reformed. This points to the weakness of any mission strategy
that would focus exclusively on the Reformed. Figures are available at: http://www.
nepszamlalas.hu/hun/kotetek/05/tables/prnt3_2.html (April 27, 2006).

the framework of a denominational culture without the need to become cross-cultural. Pastoral leadership is shaped by the patterns taken from an age when the church ministered in a radically different context. Its basic focus is maintaining the life and ministry of the church. That leadership is carried out in the more rural, traditional, Christendom paradigm, being unable to shape churches that could engage the secular, urban and global culture with the gospel. Maintenance oriented leadership operates with a vision of the church of the passing Christendom.

The second response becoming more and more tangible is the pastoral leaders' search for working methods, programmes and models. This approach is called the pragmatic, functional or managerial mission model in this study. Its presupposition is that introducing the right methods and finding the appropriate ways of how to do ministry will guide the church out of the mission crisis. I have heard about a small, rural town church that utilizes Willow Creek materials, while the number of churches starting Alpha Courses is growing fast, and Klaus Douglass' *The New Reformation* is widely discussed.[10] In the hope of finding a model, a method, or a programme that works, one can easily engage with the problems on a pragmatic, superficial level without asking the more important questions of our specific context and challenges that are present behind the perceivable crisis of mission and leadership in the city.

In the context, when old, traditional forms of ministry prove to be irrelevant and ineffective, and the ready-made models and methods seem to be inadequate, a third missiological response is proposed. The missional leader identifies as a transformational leader, rather than a person of maintenance, and is willing to understand a changed urban context and to think contextually and creatively about new forms of ministry. Missional leadership is pastoral leadership that grows out of a missional understanding of the church and its calling in the world. That approach is not sufficed by looking into the past or by applying superficial methods, but calls for shaping missional communities in the city.

---

10. Klaus Douglass, *Az új reformáció* (The New Reformation) (Budapest: Kálvin Kiadó, 2002).

The Missional Church

The North American *Gospel and Our Culture Network* introduced to a wide audience the term 'missional church'.[11] It emphasizes that the church's essential nature is to be found in being sent by God into the world, underlining the church's essentially missionary nature. George Hunsberger emphasizes that there must be a three-level permanent dialogue in the missional church in order to bring about a missionary encounter with the culture.[12] The following diagram helps to envision this dialogue:

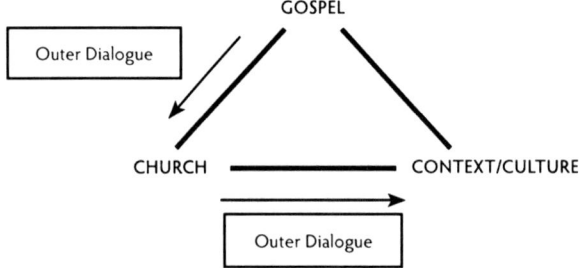

Missional ecclesiology has three main focuses: culture analysis, gospel discernment, and church renewal/change. Hunsberger argues that we often reduce the gospel and culture issue to a dialogue between two parties, and position ourselves, the church, on the gospel side.[13] We would be willing to take the comfortable place of the outsider as we look at the culture. However, the way we, the church, understand God and the gospel is culturally bound, thus our understanding is always partial. We are also part of the culture and that makes it senseless to assume that we could witness to the gospel in our own context in an objective way. Hunsberger further clarifies the character of this dialogue: ". . . the gospel's first-order encounter with the culture we inhabit will be with us, not with any 'them' out there.

---

11. See the groundbreaking book: Darrell L. Guder ed., *Missional Church: A Vision for the Sending of the Church in North America* (Grand Rapids: Eerdmans, 1998). For a summary of their understanding of missional ecclesiology, see pp. 11–12.

12. George R. Hunsberger, "Acquiring the Posture of a Missionary Church", in *The Church Between Gospel and Culture: The Emerging Mission in North America* ed. by George R. Hunsberger, and Craig Van Gelder (Grand Rapids: Eerdmans, 1996), pp. 289–297.

13. Ibid, p. 295.

The encounter is first of all an inner dialogue before it is an outer one."[14] After that internal dialogue, that is the gospel's transforming engagement with us, the church becomes the 'hermeneutic of the gospel' as it enters the outer dialogue with the gospel. Thus the church should seek her identity, as God's sent people, in both sides: "we stand on the culture side, encountered there by the gospel that engages the culture first as an inner dialogue with us; and we stand on the gospel side, called to be the visible hermeneutic of the gospel in and for its encounter with the culture."[15]

This is the missiological-theological understanding on which I have built my courses.

The Methodology and the Content of the Courses

The Stated Goals of the Course

The syllabus presented the following aims: 1) to introduce the student into the relevant issues of urban mission and pastoral leadership; 2) to expose the student to models of housing estate churches in Budapest, and through that, to help the development of critical-analytical attitudes and skills; 3) to offer biblical and sociological knowledge assisting ministry and mission in housing estates; 4) to explore the need and methods of empowering church members for ministry; and 5) to foster personal reflection on whether the student can think of him or herself as being involved in urban and/or housing estate ministry in the future.

Methodology and Assignments

Harvey Conn and Manuel Ortiz argue that leadership training should not be exclusively based on the classroom setting of seminaries, where the student is considered 'merely a container to be filled'.[16] Rather, they call for a context specific church-based training, which takes what is already there – an individual with potential for leadership – and further develops

---

14. Ibid, p. 295.
15. Ibid, pp. 296–297.
16. Harvey M. Conn and Manuel Ortiz, *Urban Ministry* (Downers Grove, IL: IVP, 2001), p. 415.

the student. That approach implies that a curriculum for urban leaders should be flexible and dynamic, so that it can be adjusted to the specific situation of the leader. In that model the leader is not removed from his or her ministry context as in traditional seminary training. Rather, the leader is encouraged to learn by example and doing (being mentored). As to the content of an urban curriculum, Conn and Ortiz propose that it should be designed with keeping the mutual interaction of three components (context, mission, student) in mind:

> All three components interact with each other as we continually evaluate each one in light of the other two. The student learns how to carry out a mission while continually assessing whether or not the mission task is appropriate for the context. The student will also ask whether his or her gifts are appropriate for the mission. All the components and their mutual shaping must continually be evaluated in the light of Scripture.[17]

It was evident that an elective course that extended thirteen weeks, which was one semester, could not induce transformation of seminary training in the HRC. The basic elements, like classroom settings and students taken out of the ministry contexts, were given. Still, my effort was to design a course that took the insights mentioned above seriously; thus, the course not only had lectures and presentations, but also church visits. As part of their assignments students were required to prepare a paper researching and analyzing one ministry area of a housing estate church. The students were to select the church and the ministry they were interested in.[18] Then they observed the actual ministry if it was possible. It was suggested that they did an interview with the pastor or another leader involved in the

---

17. Ibid., p. 421. See also Van Engen's overview of traditional theological education and proposal for the new paradigm of 'in-ministry formation' in: Charles Van Engen, *Mission on the Way: Issues in Mission Theology* (Grand Rapids: Baker Books, 1996), pp. 241–252. See also Guder in *Missional Church*, pp. 212–220.

18. A list of churches and ministry areas was provided, however students could find and work on issues identified by themselves.

selected ministry area. The students not only described what they had observed, but were expected to prepare an analysis of that ministry in the light of the housing estate context, the gospel, and the church's functions. Finally, the paper had to have a concluding paragraph containing personal reflections, possibility of application and identifying future challenges.[19] It was assumed that this approach would help the students to develop critical and analytical skills and to start thinking contextually about mission on the housing estate.

These three methodological elements – exposing students to real ministry experiences, having them prepare a paper based on analyzing the context, gospel understanding and church ministry, and encouraging them to carry out personal reflection on their calling, strengths and weaknesses – was also part of the *Church Planting in Urban Context* course. As part of this learning experience we spent three days in Amsterdam getting to know the *Amsterdam on the Move for Jesus Christ* church-planting network.[20]

The Content of the Course

The course started by outlining missional ecclesiology in the present missional crisis of the HRC. The class discussed the three-party dialogue of gospel, culture and church as it is demonstrated in the work of Lesslie Newbigin and the *Gospel and Our Culture Network*. Then the following topics were presented and discussed:

1. The sociological context of housing estates in Hungary.
2. What is the gospel? The biblical foundations of holistic mission.
3. The possibility of Christian community development on the housing estate.
4. Urban youth ministry.
5. The birth and development of the housing estate church.
6. Pastoral leadership in the missional church.
7. Training and empowering leaders in the missional church.

---

19. The following questions guide the students in personal reflection: Can you imagine yourself in urban ministry/church planting in the future? Why or why not? What are your strengths and weaknesses in light of urban ministry? What should you do in the future to better prepare yourself for urban ministry/church planting?

20. See: http://amsterdam-inbeweging.nl (24 July 2013)

8. Evangelistic methods – the Alpha Course.
9. The worship service of the missional church.
10. The missional leader's spirituality.

Relevant Issues from My Experience

In the last part of this paper, first I review some characteristic feedback by students[21] and then summarize my conclusions regarding theological education.

Students' Feedback

Students experienced a transformation of what we call missional vision. One says she received a new and very important perspective. Her discovery has been that Christians live in a missional situation: "That was the first time I realized . . . that today's missional situation was similar to the time of the first Christians. The world is essentially pagan." She goes on to say that many of us, included herself, are surprised when somebody does not understand our words in the so-called Christian Europe. She had to discover that these are new and unknown thoughts for many.

A new understanding of the contextual nature of ministry has been developed in another student. She emphasizes that during this course was the first time she had discovered that even two villages are not the same; thus it is essential that a pastor should research the context where he or she is called to minister. Then she adds: "I think that all that we have heard in class is useful in all kinds of ministry, not exclusively in housing estate mission. I feel that if I happen to be a pastor in a village I will be able to apply a lot of what I have learned."

Another student's understanding of mission and pastoral ministry also demonstrates signs of transformation. He says that before the course he would have emphasized new methods for mission and ministry, and these are exactly what he expected to learn about in the class. To illustrate

---

21. Based on interviews which were done as part of my Doctor of Ministry dissertation, and also from written student evaluations of the course *Church Planting in Urban Context.*

this expectation, he names the Alpha Course, refers to Rick Warren's *Purpose Driven Life*, and mentions introducing music that contemporary people would like. He speaks of a church he is involved with where the above-mentioned methods are applied, with results, but he feels that the expectations of the modern age are the main driving force behind these. After the course, however, he found missional spirituality more important – an attitude to mission that is embodied in his desire to take part in what God is doing: "Missional spirituality captured me. . . . Regarding the growth of the congregation it is more important to stand in the work of God [than applying methods]." He further explains that each method was developed and became successful in a specific context, often in a foreign one, and thus needs to be adapted to the Hungarian context.

The notion of spirituality also appears. One student writes in the survey referring to a class taught by a guest speaker: "I have made a resolution: to wholly deal with my own spiritual and emotional wounds and problems before I become a pastor."

Some further remarks by students on the church-planting course follow:

> When I chose the seminar I was almost convinced that I would never feel called to be involved in church planting or urban mission. Still, I felt some irresistible desire to learn about these ministries. The more I learned, the more material, books and articles I read concerning these themes, the more I owned this mission. The Amsterdam journey has become almost a spiritual renewal to me. My thinking and my faith have been deeply impacted by what I experienced there. It has been a long time since I experienced such an intensive spiritual and intellectual transformation.

> The Amsterdam visit has been a real learning experience for me – not from the tourist's perspective but from the student's. . . . The city's special part is the red light district. Facing prostitution and drugs first shocked me on a personal level, but also as a student of theology. The question immediately appeared: how is it possible to proclaim the gospel here – how can Scripture have a voice in this place? I am glad that this

question came to me early in our visit, on Friday morning, since it followed me the whole weekend. Later I saw a number of answers and examples, and finally I closed the issue in a very positive frame of mind. This became the illustration of the fact that the gospel knows no boundaries, and it can grow in any kind of environment. Though this growth happens in different ways in different contexts.

To see the power of the gospel in a world in which nothing binds people to the church anymore, where humanly speaking nobody has any profit from the religious community, has been an incredible experience. I think we have precious examples before us showing that God still has a plan for people, and our responsibility is to invite those people into his plan.

One of the most important things I recognized is the missional perspective: to see that the city, the church, one district or the other is primarily not my working area but God's.

Some Concluding Remarks

My experiences point to the usefulness and efficiency of an integrating model in training for church leadership.

Integrating church and world. The missiological approach, understanding and entering the three-party dialogue of gospel, church and context, seems to have opened new perspectives and vision for potential leaders. My conviction is that this missiological approach should permeate the whole spectrum of seminary training – not having it confined to practical theology disciplines. Everything is to be taught and examined in the dynamic of the gospel, culture and church. This approach provides students a tool that helps them to grapple with the issues of a fast-changing world where new ministry challenges emerge continually.

Integrating denominational commitment/identity and openness to other forms of ministry. Experiencing new forms of ministry, which are done in different styles by different denominations and in one case in a different country, has powerfully opened up the theological vision of the students.

My suggestion is that students should be exposed frequently to ministry models that are not familiar to them. It requires the teaching of skills that help them critically reflect on their experiences. Theological students in HRC are to transcend the unhealthy dichotomy of evaluating ministries as totally good or bad, which is often not different from 'our kind' and 'not Reformed'.

Integrating the personal/spiritual and the academic. Introducing spiritual reflection and having students search for the personal dimensions of what they were actually studying seems to have been a fruitful experiment. Seminary training should be much more conscious and open about seeking the opportunities and forms of integrating the academic and personal dimensions.

Bibliography

Amsterdam in Bewegin voor Jezus Christus. AiB. http://amsterdam-inbeweging. nl (24 July 2013).

Conn, Harvey M. and Manuel Ortiz. *Urban Ministry.* Downers Grove, IL: IVP, 2001.

Douglass, Klaus. *Az új reformáció* (The New Reformation). Budapest: Kálvin Kiadó, 2002.

Engen, Charles van. *Mission on the Way: Issues in Mission Theology.* Grand Rapids: Baker Books, 1996.

Fazakas, Sándor. Új *egyház felé? A második világháború utáni református egyházi megújulás ekkléziológiai konzekvenciái* ("Towards a new church?" The Ecclesiological Consequences of the Reformed Church Renewal after the Second World War). Debrecen: Debreceni Református Kollégium, 2000.

Guder, Darrell L., ed. *Missional Church: A Vision for the Sending of the Church in North America.* Grand Rapids: Eerdmans, 1998.

Hunsberger, George R. "Acquiring the Posture of a Missionary Church", in George R. Hunsberger, and Craig Van Gelder, *The Church Between Gospel and Culture: The Emerging Mission in North America.* Grand Rapids: Eerdmans, 1996, pp. 289–297.

Központi Statisztikai Hivatal. Népszamlàlàs. http://www.nepszamlalas.hu/hun/ kotetek/05/tables/prnt3_2.html (April 27, 2006).

Szabó, István Bogárdi. "Az MRE elmúlt tíz *évének írásos értékelései*", *THÉMA* 3, No. 1 (2001): p. 14–27.

CHAPTER 5

A Growing Need for a Common Moral Vision: A Cry for Humble Co-operation between Theology and Other Disciplines

István Pásztori-Kupán

I argue in this paper that while the planet is running towards a social and ecological disaster, the influential public actors, including the theologians, have been nurturing their own illusions. The political classes hoped to discover the answer for the environmental crisis in the illusory idea of 'sustainable development'. Scientists avoided the responsibility by referring to 'scientific neutrality'. Theology itself often followed a similarly illusory self definition by considering itself as 'the conscience' of other sciences.

However, the present economic crisis, caused primarily by moral decline, wakes us all from our illusions. It is a clear consequence of our interdependence as scholars that from an ethical perspective scientists, economists, politicians, etc., can never be neutral: this moral responsibility can neither be devolved to others, nor taken over from them. Philosophy should not be a handmaid, but rather the ally of theology for the sake of the *homo ethicus*.

All are One?

Our way of life influences both directly and indirectly all other creatures of the earth. As the capacity of living rationally and reflecting on our influence on other creatures of the planet is a characteristic exclusive of the human race, we have a non-negligible and non-transferable responsibility for our shared habitat. The question becomes unavoidable: are we able to live responsibly or are we merely living as tyrants and parasites on a sensitive planet, which is neither infinite, nor indestructible?

'All are one' according to Heraclitus. This ancient wisdom drew attention to the interdependence of all things. This idea has its resonances in the New Testament, too.

Paul, speaking in front of the Stoic and Epicurean philosophers in Athens, reminds us that God has made all nations 'of one blood', determining beforehand their times and the bounds of their habitation. Interestingly enough, in order to emphasize the mutual interdependence of all people who had descended from 'the one', Paul does not quote the Old Testament, but rather the Cilician poet Aratus, according to whom we are 'God's offspring'.[1]

In the New Testament the term *patria* denotes 'nation' or 'race' (see Luke 2:4, Acts 3:25, Eph 3:14–15). Nevertheless, in post-biblical times – and perhaps not without the influence of Acts 17:26 – the term also came to be used in the sense of *habitat*, as an inheritance received by humankind from the *Pater* (i.e. the Father). This is where the Indo-European words *patria* and *patrimonium* as well as the German term *Vaterland* derive from.[2]

Therefore, all is one, or at least, according to the biblical teaching, all originate from and gain the inheritance from the same father. Yet, seen from the perspective of two millennia, have we actually grown to bear the responsibility of this honour? The on-going military confrontations, the exclusively profit-oriented industrialization and the insatiability of multinational companies keep tearing apart both our societies and the

---

1. See Acts 17:26–28.

2. The Hungarian language uses the expression 'motherland' showing the close connection between human beings and the world: the *mother* is from whom one gains his/her *matter* (in Latin, *mater* is the source of *materia*).

earth. In today's fragmented world we need to learn the lesson of unity again, since due to the globalization all our decisions and actions affect the lives of others who may live on the opposite side of this small planet.

Sustainable Development: Plans and Illusions

Another way of defining our responsibility towards the earth and each other is that we do not simply inherit our habitat from our ancestors, but rather borrow it from our children.[3] In the name of universal human solidarity, the above admonition brings every human generation to trial not only in front of the Lord of history, but also before the court of their descendants. The future of our children and grandchildren is decided now: we recklessly participate in the formation of their fate, even with our indolence. Perhaps it has never been so crucial whether the current generation is actually able to preserve its inheritance and pass it on by living consciously in order to prevent their grandchildren from fighting over drinking water. At this point we are unmistakably faced with the biblical challenge of feeding the five thousand with five loaves and two fish.[4]

Whenever I discuss with my students the inequality and injustice that are so unmistakably present in our world, I usually refer to a satellite image on the NASA webpage of our planet at night. The presence and absence of artificial lights shows exactly where the Orwellian 'equals' and 'the more equals' live.[5]

Economics and politics offer the global remedy for such problems in the idea of 'sustainable development'. This idea is contained in the so-called *Bruntland Report* (1987) of the United Nations. According to its definition,

---

3. Cf. Mawis Lewis-Webber, "Young Children and Environmental Ethics", *Environmental Education at the Early Childhood Level*, ed. by Ruth A. Wilson (Troy: North American Association for Environmental Education, 1994), pp. 23–27.

4. John 6:1–15.

5. http://apod.nasa.gov/apod/ap001127.html, viewed on 18 May 2011. Cf. George Orwell, *Animal Farm*, Chapter 10: "All animals are equal, but some animals are more equal than others."

> Sustainable development is development that meets the needs
> of the present without compromising the ability of future
> generations to meet their own needs.[6]

Unfortunately, the continuation is not very encouraging, since according to the document, the idea of sustainable development contains within it two key concepts: the concept of 'needs', in particular the essential needs of the world's poor to which overriding priority should be given; and the idea of limitations imposed by the state of technology and social organization on the environment's ability to meet present and future needs.[7]

It was clear already at the time of the report's formulation, that the 'needs' of the present largely exceed the limited resources of our planet, because the 'needs' of humankind are increasingly dictated by the profit-oriented market. This wildly strengthening *dictatorship of artificial and market-centred needs* or rather 'claims' is in total contradiction with the requirements of a responsible attitude towards the next generation. It is *artificial*, because it generates unreal needs;[8] it is *market-centred*, because it is based exclusively on profit-making without any ethical bounds;[9] and it is a *dictatorship*, because it enters mercilessly into the everyday life and home of every family and social class.[10]

The first concept puts forward the essential need of the world's poor, which is indeed commendable. Nevertheless, the biggest problem with the second statement is that the subject of the sentence is 'the state of technology and social organization' and not 'the environment' itself. According to the

---

6. *UN Report of the World Commission on Environment and Development: Our Common Future*, Part I, Chapter II: Towards Sustainable Development. http://www.un-documents. net/ocf-02.htm, accessed on 18 May 2013.

7. Ibid., Part I, Chapter II.

8. E.g. it makes a seven-year-old child believe that he/she desperately 'needs' a mobile phone equipped with the latest multimedia extras on the market.

9. In an exclusively profit-oriented commerce the question whether one should sell a refrigerator to the Eskimos does not even occur. Instead, only one thing matters: how can I persuade the Eskimos to buy this product?

10. E.g. the young children already in possession of a multimedia mobile phone often ostracize those who do not have one. The children who want to be accepted by their classmates, approach their parents with the claim (which they consider entirely justified), thus introducing inevitably the dictatorship of the market and of fashion into the life of the family.

logic of this affirmation, the state of technology and social organization defines the limits of the ecosystem regarding the satisfaction of human needs, and not the ecosystem itself. The document which originated from within the so called consumer-society tries to avoid the unavoidable: within its opening statement it does not state clearly that we have to adapt and adjust our real needs to the possibilities of the planet and not vice versa. It is not the technology, but the environment itself that sets the limits of our possibilities: the inexistent cannot be exploited. The document attempts to make the notion of sustainable development believable by the progress of various technologies and worldwide social justice, without facing the decisive question: do we actually need everything we have or we are claiming we need? Further: do we need everything we have in such quantities? Do we need everything so frequently? The unsustainable character of such development derives exactly from the relentlessness of the market's dictatorship.

Two and a half decades before the proclamation of the above UN document, on 10 July 1963, President John Fitzgerald Kennedy affirmed in his commencement address at the American University:

> In the final analysis, our most basic common link is that we all inhabit this small planet. We all breathe the same air. We all cherish our children's future. And we are all mortal.[11]

Kennedy's thoughts are commendable. It is evident from the above that one cannot even begin to think about the future of our planet and of humankind without a thorough ethical reflection. This must begin with the inescapable redefinition of our needs and claims, but not according to the demands of the market, but rather in light of our responsibility towards our descendants and this small 'patria' of all. Only this process may facilitate the formation and strengthening of a truly Christian, human and environmental ethics, realizable by a conscious change in our habits. The education of a generation with a strong sense of responsibility for the next

---

11. John F. Kennedy, *Commencement Address at American University*, Washington, DC, 10 June 1963. http://www.humanity.org/voices/commencements/speeches/index. php?page=jfk_at_american, accessed on 18 May 2013.

ones cannot be successful without the development of a morally correct attitude vis-à-vis another human being and the environment.

The Illusion of Moral Development

As is demonstrated by the entire history of humankind and especially by the whole of the twentieth century, we must give up the illusion of 'sustainable development' not only in the economical but also in ethical sense. Those ideas of the Enlightenment according to which the introduction of universal education will result in global happiness, and the spreading of knowledge and science will produce an ever-increasing morality, were proven to be illusions. The moral flaws of human beings are more fundamental than the Enlightenment philosophers envisaged.

Even without invoking the affirmations of theological anthropology regarding the basic nature of human beings, we may safely conclude that there has not been any substantial improvements on the moral level within humankind during the past two thousand and especially during the last one hundred years. The school history manuals often present the slavery of the age of Pericles as one of the 'flaws' of ancient Greek democracy. Nevertheless, based on the demonstrative lesson of history, we should know by now that slavery is not merely a flaw or a stain, but rather an indispensable accessory of democracy. The only important difference is that while the people of the ancient polis honestly acknowledged this fact and the masters lived together with their slaves (even at times under the same roof), today we strive to keep our slaves on other continents so as not to be disturbed by their mere presence. Our democracy is certainly more presentable, yet not peculiarly more human than those of old: ever so often it merely neutralizes our moral sensibility with the required elegance. The celebrated enlightenment rationality thus easily leads to inhuman solutions.

The Illusion of a Morally Neutral Science

The notion of *scientific neutrality* is not only present, but often plays a crucial role in our time. This usually involves the idea that through its objective methods science formulates its valid affirmations concerning the analyzed reality, presenting the discoveries and developments. Moreover, with political help it may also introduce its innovations. During these processes the ethical responsibility does not always burden the scientist. Nonetheless, my rationale in this matter is the following:

1. Science and knowledge are power.
2. The cultivation of science is an exercise of power.
3. The exercise of power involves moral accountability.
4. Any moral accountability resulting from the exercise of power is inevitable and non-transferable, including the assumption of responsibility for any consequences.

Thus, if anyone discovers and makes atomic energy available, he or she has to take into account that this innovation can be used not only for production, but also for terrible destruction. For example, atomic scientists as well as geneticists cannot and should not avoid extremely serious moral dilemmas. Their recurrent ethical problem is that with political support they can obtain a substantial income even at the cost of jeopardizing the health of the population either by improperly used atomic energy or by the production of genetically modified foods and plants. I think that the affirmation of J. Robert Oppenheimer, the 'father' of the first atomic bomb, is still worthy of our consideration:

> The physics which played the decisive part in the development of the atomic bomb came straight out of our laboratories and our journals. Despite the vision and the far-seeing wisdom of our wartime heads of state, the physicists felt a peculiarly intimate responsibility for suggesting, for supporting, and in the end, in large measure, for achieving the realization of atomic weapons. Nor can we forget that these weapons, as they were in fact used, dramatized so mercilessly the inhumanity and evil of modern war. In some sort of crude sense which no

vulgarity, no humour, no over-statement can quite extinguish, the physicists have known sin; and this is a knowledge which they cannot lose.[12]

One of the most crucial messages of this shocking text is that Oppenheimer chooses to define the moral responsibility of atomic scientists neither by juridical nor by psychological terms. He does not speak of 'error', 'mistake', 'fault' or 'misconduct', but rather uses an unmistakable and extremely laden theological expression when he says that "the physicists have known *sin*", and regardless of how they would desire to get rid of it, this knowledge is now inseparable from them. They cannot and perhaps should not lose this knowledge. This is a huge memento as well as a powerful prophetic warning.

We can draw similar conclusions from the recent history of scientific economics. The most distinguished economic universities of the world have published manuals in order to prevent the economic crises.[13] It was interesting to observe that behind the almost fatal collapse of the world economy which started on 15 September 2008, there were numerous specialists and businessmen who had previously spoken about various methods to prevent such disasters.[14] Again, the conclusion is the same: scientific methods in themselves are not enough. Science without a robust morality inevitably fails in the long run.

Upon analyzing the future of life and humankind, the health of our planet as well as the expected moral and human behaviour of the next generations, the scientific responsibility – or better said, the lack of the

---

12. J. Robert Oppenheimer, "Physics in the Contemporary World", in *Arthur Dehon Little memorial lecture at the Massachusetts Institute of Technology*, 25 November 1947 (Cambridge, MA, 1947). Cf. J. Robert Oppenheimer, "Physics in the Contemporary World", in *Bulletin of the Atomic Scientists* Vol. 4, No. 3 (March 1948), pp. 65–68 and pp. 85–86 (p. 66). In his interview given to *Time* magazine he also expressed himself in the same manner. See "Expiation," *Time*, p. 94 (23 February 1948), http://www.time.com/time/magazine/article/0,9171,798265,00.html, accessed on 18 May 2013.

13. See e.g. *Harvard Business Review on Crisis Management* (Boston: Harvard Business School Press, 2000). The first edition of the work appeared in 1994.

14. The reality is certainly more complex and troubling than that which was revealed in the 2010 documentary entitled *Inside Job*. See http://www.imdb.com/title/tt1645089/, viewed on 18 May 2013.

assumption of responsibility by the sciences and scientists – can easily have devastating consequences. The typical question of the twentieth and twenty-first centuries – the recurrent "Why not?", "Why should we not do this or that simply because we are capable of doing it?" – can lead humankind and life itself to destruction. The enormous amount of new technology introduced often within uncontrolled circumstances or based on falsified experimental data, the ever-deepening chasm between 'equals' and 'more equals' make us realize that we have a deficit on the level of conscious moral education, and that the public immorality is gradually becoming the contemporary ethos, thus threatening to eliminate our stimulus-threshold of morality which could still move us upon seeing the need of others and the injustices they suffer. One of the worrying results of our waning morality is that by merely reading or watching the daily news we come to accept more and more terrible things as commonplaces. These anomalies, which derive also from the immorality of pseudo-scientific behaviour, can only be annihilated on the social level by a serious ethical education of responsible, grown-up citizens.

The scientists and sciences of our time must do away once and for all with any pseudo-scientific illusion concerning concepts like 'moral neutrality'. Just as the dissemination of knowledge is a moral duty of all scholars and researchers, in the same manner it is their obligation to assess the possible short-term and long-term effects of all discoveries and innovations. The decision concerning the methods, the conditions and limits of introduction of such novelties should be made according to these previous assessments, and not by purposefully circumventing or ignoring the foreseeable consequences. The ethicists of the relevant science should primarily carry out this evaluation and weighing.

Nonetheless, we obviously find ourselves in the situation that ethics are usually trudging behind the rapidly developing science, and therefore its cautious warnings are often characterized as 'posterior wisdom' (i.e. locking the stable-door after the horse has bolted).[15] It turns out again

---

15. In the world of economics see e.g. Joseph L. Badaracco, Jr., *Business Ethics: Roles and Responsibilities* (Homewood, IL: Richard D. Irwin Inc., 1994); Max H. Bazerman and Ann E. Tenbrunsel, *Blind Spots: Why We Fail to Do What's Right and What to Do About It* (Princeton: Princeton University Press, 2011); George C. Lodge and Craig Wilson, *A*

and again that our ethical vision was not broad enough to envisage the approaching disaster.

Therefore, it could be claimed that while the average member of society followed the illusion of a sustainable development without any self-control or self-limitation and began to live more and more irresponsibly, there is a serious moral crisis which is responsible for both our economic and environmental problems. This moral crisis appears in different forms at the levels of middle class, scientists, politicians, and businessmen. It plays a key role everywhere in the irresponsible thirst for profit, in the individual prodigality and refusal to reassess one's true needs, and in the inhuman attitude which does not take into account the fate of others.

A Possible Synergy between Theological Ethics and Sciences

Theological ethics could not escape its own peculiar illusions either for a considerably long time. Systematic theologians did not indulge themselves as much in the myths of 'scientific neutrality' or 'sustainable development', but had to face the rather self-deceptive idea that theological ethics is the conscience of all other sciences. From this frequent starting point derived a certain heroic effort by which modern theologians strove to reflect ethically upon all those phenomena, which had been either neglected or merely touched upon by ethicists of other sciences. One of the obvious disadvantages of this process was the visibly increased unpopularity of theologians. See, for example, the not always unfounded assertions like "the theologians pretend to know it all". The theologians who are truly concerned about humankind and the world have to understand that our duty is not to work on the morals of science and society *instead* of other scientists, but rather *together with* them.

Corporate Solution to Global Poverty: How Multinationals Can Help the Poor and Invigorate Their Own Legitimacy (Princeton: Princeton University Press, 2006); Lynn S. Paine, *Cases in Leadership, Ethics, and Organizational Integrity: A Strategic Perspective* (Burr Ridge, IL: Richard D. Irwin, 1997); Sandra J. Sucher, *The Moral Leader: Challenges, Tools, and Insights* (New York: Routledge, 2007).

The fact that the contemporary crisis has a profoundly ethical origin wakes us all up from our various illusions. As a natural consequence of this, we have to assert that science and the scientist can never be neutral in a moral sense. This moral responsibility can not be devolved to others, or taken over from them. As ethicists of different sciences we are interdependent. The theologians of our age – regardless of how much they would love it – cannot propose to themselves to formulate the ethics of the oil industry, car manufacturing, genetic engineering, waste management, etc. It is nonetheless our common and scientific task to consolidate within our disciples and students all those behavioural patterns by which, at the behest of their own social, human and environmental morality, they themselves shall be able to formulate and follow these ethical rules as scientists, politicians or any other members of the society.

Further, the Christian theological anthropology is ignorant of a 'sustainable development' in the moral sense. Despite the fact that there had been attempts within theology, which sought to accomplish 'God's Kingdom' on earth by a gradual moral elevation of humankind, these ideas were always refuted not only by human history, but also by the very history of Christianity itself. This assertion does not necessarily mean that we agree with Max Weber's thesis concerning the spirit of capitalism.[16] Nevertheless, it is undeniable that the human being was not improved in a moral sense either by the universal and compulsory education, or by the rapidly developing sciences, technologies and the series of comfort-increasing services of modern civilization. As a theologian I must add with repentance: man was not bettered by the often self-emptied moralizing sermons either.

In an attempt to sum it up, we may assert that the moral vision of scientists, politicians and economists has often been far too narrow and far too simple to prevent the tragedies. This necessitates a more robust and complex moral vision for our globalized, and also very complex, world. It is also true that theology in itself is incapable of providing such a detailed moral vision. Therefore, it is time for the ethicists of various fields

---

16. Max Weber, Die Protestantische Ethik und der Geist des Kapitalismus (Tübingen: Mohr, 1934).

(economists, scientists, political and health experts, physicists, theologians, etc.) to start working together by breaking the barriers of 'scientific overspecialization', which separate and even isolate us from each other. Thus, by a conscious determination to learn from each other, through a real and common effort, we may be able to formulate and provide a moral vision suitable indeed for our present and future. Theology could assist this project, *inter alia*, by its recurrent emphasis upon the perspective beyond the material world, evincing the inadequacy of the idea of a sustainable, yet merely material development.

Our work is not little, since we have to revive and refine within the whole of the society all those ethical sensibilities and mechanisms, which were largely corrupted by the dictatorship of artificial and exclusively market-oriented 'needs'. Before the dangerously spreading moral neutrality deteriorates into moral indifference, the responsible specialists of various sciences ought to pinpoint by a serious collaboration all the problems underlying social phenomena, working conditions, production, education, healthcare, consumption, energy management and human relationships, and ought to formulate ethically valid responses to these. This in itself is already our inevitable, non-transferable and common scientific responsibility. As a theologian I would conclude with the very words by which Jesus challenges our moral commitment: "Blessed are the meek, for they shall inherit the earth" (Matt 5:5).

Bibliography

Augustine, Norman R. et al. *Harvard Business Review on Crisis Management.* Boston: Harvard Business School Press, 2000.

Badaracco, Joseph L., Jr. *Business Ethics: Roles and Responsibilities.* Homewood, IL: Richard D. Irwin Inc., 1994.

Bazerman, Max H. and Ann E. Tenbrunsel. *Blind Spots: Why We Fail to Do What's Right and What to Do About It.* Princeton: Princeton University Press, 2011.

Ferguson, Charles. *Inside Job.* Directed by Charles Ferguson. New York: Sony Pictures Classics, 2010 (viewed on 18 May 2013).

Kennedy, John F. *Commencement Address at American University*, Washington, DC, 10 June 1963. Available through http://www.humanity.org/voices/

commencements/speeches/index.php?page=jfk_at_american (Accessed on 18 May 2013).

Lewis-Webber, Mawis. "Young Children and Environmental Ethics", in: Ruth A. Wilson (ed.) *Environmental Education at the Early Childhood Level.* Troy: North American Association for Environmental Education, 1994, pp. 23–27.

Lodge, George C. and Craig Wilson. *A Corporate Solution to Global Poverty: How Multinationals Can Help the Poor and Invigorate Their Own Legitimacy.* Princeton: Princeton University Press, 2006.

Nemiroff, Robert and Jerry Bonnell. "Astronomy picture of the day". Earth at night. November 27, 2000. Available through http://apod.nasa.gov/apod/ap001127.html (Accessed on 18 May 2011).

Oppenheimer, J. Robert. "Physics in the Contemporary World", in *Arthur Dehon Little memorial lecture at the Massachusetts Institute of Technology*, 25 November 1947 (Cambridge, MA, 1947).

———. "Physics in the Contemporary World", in *Bulletin of the Atomic Scientists,* Vol. 4, No. 3 (March 1948): pp. 65–68 and pp. 85–86

Orwell, George. *Animal Farm.* London: Penguin Classics, 2000.

Paine, Lynn S. *Cases in Leadership, Ethics, and Organizational Integrity: A Strategic Perspective.* Burr Ridge, IL: Richard D. Irwin, 1997.

Sucher, Sandra J. *The Moral Leader: Challenges, Tools, and Insights.* New York: Routledge, 2007.

Time magazine. "Science: Expiation", *Time*, February 23, 1948, available through http://www.time.com/time/magazine/article/0,9171,798265,00.html (Accessed on 18 May 2013).

UN Report of the World Commission on Environment and Development: Our Common Future, Part 1, Chapter II: Towards Sustainable Development. http://www.un-documents.net/ocf-02.htm (Accessed on 18 May 2013).

Weber, Max. Die Protestantische Ethik und der Geist des Kapitalismus. Tübingen: Mohr, 1934.

CHAPTER 6

The Place of the Theological Academy in the Church: A Case for Public Theology

Tamás Béres

The relationship between church and academy is often held as a source of tension and problems. I admit that academy lies in the intersection of church-related and secular establishments and this situation can easily cause a certain tension. Nevertheless, I want to argue that this is more an opportunity than a problem. In the following article I first present a survey of the relationship between church, academy, and society. I also investigate briefly the tension which springs from this relationship. As a second step I will argue that pursuing public theology may be the key for turning this tension into fruitful concepts for both secular and church-related society.

The Church – How Christians Live Together

In many countries most Christians live their religious life in an organized way. Where they have the opportunity and do not lack fundamental freedom, they regularly meet together, form communities, and gather at places of worship – just like in biblical times. Living as a Christian implies living in community. But living in community is not the main hallmark of a Christian life. It is, rather, forming congregations.

I want to emphasize congregations (*congregatio*, *Versammlung*) instead of communities (*communio*, *Gemeinde*) with a good reason. The ability of congregations to unite people comes not from the work of their members but from the words of the gospel and from the power of the sacraments, that is, in a final sense from Jesus Christ. Of course, it must be a permanent aim of a congregation to build and develop communities within the church, where people truly want to carry each other's burdens and joys. However, what always has to be preserved is an openness towards inquiring people from the outside. It is a crucial theological point that this openness can never be realized through community building exercises or through using excellent communicational 'hi-tech', but only through the true aspiration of the members to show the love of God, the truth of God's word and the power of the sacraments. This openness towards the outside world has to be nurtured in a congregation.

Within the congregations, of course, there are Christian communities. I mean, for example, the families. The Christian family as a sociological configuration stands right on the border of the society and the church. In a sociological sense the family is a 'cell', the smallest organic and viable unit, a set of individual elements. The source of its Christian way of life is the congregational life, where family members as members of the congregation participate in the sources of God's word and the sacraments. Here they can exist in interpersonal relations, which may have special contents: telling stories and listening to narrations of others about the implications of the lifestyle of following Jesus, exchanging emotions, life experiences, etc.

Apart from congregations and communities, there are further important societal formations of Christianity that are worth mentioning. The church exists as both an organism and an organization. There were many times during church-history when representatives of both approaches had strong confrontations and quarrels regarding this question. One side of the debate emphasized the vivid and personal side of Christianity and was fed-up with problems that originated from its organizational reality (such as corruption, fighting for secular dominance, etc.). The other side wanted to emphasize the political importance of the Christian church or the holiness of its hierarchical system and tried to protect it from the confusing outcomes of individual initiatives. Some of these approaches can be present in today's church-life too, and we may meet them in everyday ecumenical encounters, at all levels. Despite this twofold experience, we have to face the fact that the church exists as an organism and an organization at the same time (cf. 1 Pet 2:5; Eph 1:23; Rom 12:4–8).

Furthermore, we have to state that the church is a virtual community as well. Church-related associations, worldwide organizations, denominations, churches, the dead and gone sisters and brothers are all under the headship of Christ, even if a real community among their members is not possible.

The Relationship between Church and Academia

The official place to train 'experts' in and for the church is usually the Theological Academy, which is customarily a part of the national system of higher education, too. It is an organizational unit of the church, where theological work is supposed to reach its highest *niveau*. The value of its theological work as an orientational background is vital for all the actors of the church-body, from the church leadership through nursing teams in hospice-work to teachers working in religious education. At the same time, the academy does not have an independent status – its work is made possible and, not least, financed by the church. Church leadership may use the academy as a scientifically authentic source to decide on theological issues, but it can also come to a decision of establishing other scientifically based theological bodies – advisory boards besides the bishops, scientific commissions on special issues, etc. Bishops are usually well-trained theological professionals, too, so they can easily decide against the establishment of any further advisory committees and thus play the role of the foremost leader both in a normative and an executive sense. Consequently, the activities of the academy intersect with those of other major representatives of the church. That is why it can cause conflicts of interests and theological interferences among the many actors of church-life. Thus, the role and place of the academy within the church is a sensitive issue.

The effectiveness of the theological work that is done in academia is often measured by extrinsic norms of academic measuring systems. This situation is the source of another tension: through the academic validation and evaluation processes the 'outer world' can enter into the church at a very substantial level, which, in many cases, may affect inner church life, too. The influence of this 'external academic system' can mean, among other things, the adoption of academic language, the acceptance of publishers, the use of standard international measurements of academic excellence and impact factors, or the harmonization of theological research with the wider system of academic institutions.

One may ask if the acceptance of such external standards has serious consequences for theological thinking, or even determines it in a certain way. Can theological work preserve 'prophetic' freedom? Can it still act out its essential and vital critical function, while it is part of a 'worldly' academic hierarchical system? Are social systems and scientific methods independent, so that by using these methods theologians are still capable of discerning important societal trends? These are legitimate questions and the issue is certainly complex, and the answers should not be simplified. Nevertheless, I still believe that theological thinking has to accept the common academic frame and basic components of contemporary academic thinking (even if not the mentality of its representatives!). Without this acceptance, it would lose its ability to meaningfully interact with contemporary concepts.

At the same time, it also has to avoid the trap of following the academic world uncritically. Theological thinking must be conscious of the nature and importance of accepted external methods but it should not forget its own traditional aspirations either. Academic method can simply overrule church context. When this happens, the purpose and nature of living-in-the-church and the performance and function of the theological work may move apart from each other. This can lead to a situation in which theology and church do not stand for each other any longer – quite the opposite, they fight against each other.[1] However, where theological work preserves its truly critical function (i.e. critical both towards the academic and the church context), such a situation should not occur.

---

1. Ingolf Dalferth, for example, makes a distinction between the 'friends of the church' and the 'friends of theology'. *Radikale Theologie* (Leipzig: Evangelische Verlagsanstalt, 2010), Einleitung.

Can the academy play an important role by preserving its ambiguities that are created by the academic nature of theology and the acceptance of the reality of the church? In such an academy, 'church' and 'world' can be seen as being in creative opposition. This ambiguity is well characterized by Christ's entering into the created world (acceptance), and dying there (antagonism) for the world (acceptance again).[2]

Academia as an Opportunity – A Special Place for the Acceptance of Global Challenges

We can state that academia, both in its structural and functional role, has all the discussed characteristics of the church:

     a)   It is a Christian congregation: God's service and worship are practiced here or these may be substituted by special occasions of lectures and seminars that have the atmosphere of transparency showing forth the divine presence.

     b)   It is a Christian community: because students, workers and co-workers form natural, societal communities in which Christian inspiration, devotion, etc., can be realized as gifts (friendships, roommates, circles of prayer, members of seminars, etc.).

     c)   It is a virtual community: academia is a part of the structural and devotional system of the church and also of higher education (e.g. people who have a concern regarding the Bologna-process, or people who read the same books and academic publications or who are interested in the same problems, etc.).

     d)   It is a living organism: the academy is where everyone can find his or her special vocation – everyone can take part in building communities together. New virtual communities can be called

---

2. L. Batka characterizes the ambiguity in the relationship of church and the 'world' (i.e. theology and society) in the following way: "A postulate of total separation of theology and society does not prove to be in accordance with the gospel, and the same can be said about the idea that they both are the one and the same 'house'." In: Lubomír Batka, "Jedes Haus, das mit sich selbst uneins ist, kann nicht bestehen." Wo begegnen sich Theologie und Gesellschaft?, In: Jens Schröter, Sophie Kottsieper (ed.), *Die Rolle der Theologie in Universitaet, Gesellschaft und Kirche* (Leipzig: Evangellische Verlagsanstalt, 2012), p. 94.

into existence or can be turned into real ones by anyone, etc.

e) It is an organization: the academy is a structural 'slice' of the church and of the higher education system. (But it also shows the characteristics of a fairly independent organizational unit.)

Consequently, not only does academia play an important role in the life of the church but it is touched, challenged and channelled in manifold ways by the life of church. However, as I argued above, it is simultaneously influenced by the life of 'external' society. This 'double citizenship' provides academia the opportunity to show theoretical and practical models for a Christian life.

The *curriculum* plays a decisive role in the mutual communication between church and academia. The process of mapping out curricula by the teaching staff of the academy is not a one-way street but rather circulates among the angles of the church-society-academy triangle. Without a firm knowledge of everyday life, as well as the problems and challenges in society and the church, academic curricula will run dry. The true value of academic knowledge depends on its relatedness to real life and its links with the life of people outside its walls.

A capacity for *managing multiple contextuality* is a challenging issue for academic theological work. The same cannot be said of the situation in the congregations, especially regarding one of their most important inner functions, namely spirituality. In an average well-organized congregation spirituality usually seems to be uniform. People that belong to it may therefore have the advantages of having a solid, clear and certain type of *common* spirituality. Congregations may have alternative theological visions, especially in a situation where there are two or more pastors or in the case of a very vivid and highly motivated congregation with many spiritual leaders, etc. But these congregations are often known more for their spiritual difficulties and troubles than for their unity. On the other hand, academia can be a place for living out the spiritual life in different ways. Pluralistic spirituality is provided by the different devotional backgrounds of students and the varieties of the theological work itself.

An Answer to Today's Worldwide Challenges: Public Theology

The academy is the special place for gathering people with a common interest of *pursuing theology* together. (One may say that theology is what we are pursued by – but emphasizing this would probably be no more than some kind of a trendy devotional sophism.) Academia can enrich the church mostly by its theological efforts and innovations. It is not in the position of the watch-keeper of the church – that is the duty of the church leadership – but it has to be able to develop critical theological views that prove usable and useful. Critical theological thinking aims at providing aspects and authentic assessments of the trends and tendencies of the actual political, cultural and economic issues for the members of the church

Earlier these aspects were emphasized by the so-called 'contextual theologies'. But as globalism won the day, the global importance of local issues became clear, because the main problems have proved to be the same all over the world. They may have different faces, but issues of poverty and wealth, righteousness and unrighteousness, justice and injustice, environmental and technical abuse, demand comprehensive answers. These issues cannot be solved only through ad hoc responses – they cry out for good theological answers and even better practical activities from the side of the church: the situation of the visible minorities and the Roma people; the disadvantageous situation of girls and women in East-Africa or Asia (who are often raped on the long roads to the water sources, or just as a symbol of oppression by men)[3]; the situation of the environment in the rich and poor countries; the economically unjust conditions of the labour market, etc., just to mention a few disgraceful global issues which are the shame of those leaders who set the local or global agendas and the trends of contemporary world processes. Christian academia has the opportunity and

---

3. This is one of the water-related issues. As the Millennium Development Goals (UN) states, the concurrence of violence and gender-related issues with the ethical consequences of uneven distribution of water on earth is one of the many serious signs of the so-called 'world *problematique*'. African and Asian girls and women spend hours per day walking to watering places. This is why girls have a great drawback in taking part in the education. Cf. Art. *Water*, in J. B. Callicott and R. Frodeman (ed.), *Encyclopedia of Environmental Ethics and Philosophy* (USA: McMillan Reference, 2009), p. 393.

obligation now to develop new and just religious and ethical standards for human coexistence, both on a critical theological and on the practical level. Theological work dealing with these questions is called Public Theology. This 'game' can only be played together, and in the present situation of the world the church urgently has to play a leading role in this serious game.

Duncan Forrester defined Public Theology in the following way: "Public Theology, as I understand it, is not primarily and directly evangelical theology which addresses the gospel to the world in the hope of repentance and conversion. Rather, it is theology which seeks the welfare of the city before protecting the interests of the church, or its proper liberty to preach the gospel and celebrate the sacraments. [. . .] It strives to offer something that is distinctive, and that is gospel, rather than simply adding the voice of theology to what everyone is saying already."[4]

While reading Forrester's words we can remember the different conceptions of St. Paul and St. Peter about the distinctive problem of early Christianity: the relationship to the world.[5] Do Christians have to care about the world outside of the church? Should they be touched and motivated by social, political and economic issues when such questions come up in the surrounding world? Public Theology is therefore a paradigm in theology, which is rooted in early Christian times in a significant way and currently getting increasing attention globally. Originally developed in the 1970s, the term 'public theology' has been used by various theologians globally – first by Reinhold Niebuhr and then David Tracy extended the term in 1981.

A new element in Public Theology is the recognition of the importance of two decisive factors: the role of new communication techniques, and mobility in cultural and social spheres. Thanks to these, global questions are right in front of our doors. In fact, they are in our houses. Major global environmental decisions have to be made right in our bathrooms

---

4. Duncan B. Forrester, "The Scope of Public Theology", *Studies in Christian Ethics*, 17 (2), 2004, p. 6.

5. How should Christians faithfully approach the surrounding profane world? The different answers to this question represented one of the basic socio-ethical conflicts of the New Testament. This can be witnessed throughout Paul and Peter's on going argument about the relationship between the *oikodomia* and *paroikia* (2 Cor 13:10; Rom 14:19; Eph 2:21 and 1 Pet 2:11).

and kitchens. The fair global economic options have to be chosen locally while doing the shopping. Better and more adequate answers are needed for a new situation that is represented by an amalgamation of religious pluralism, economic and environmental consumption, democracy, ethnic sectarianism, moral neutrality, autonomous technology, conflicting laws, etc. But these better and more adequate answers for the new global situation have to be worked out locally. Therefore, the largest worldwide net of well-organized, living, corporate structures – namely, Christianity – also has an enormous responsibility in developing these answers.

The task of Public Theology is to shed light on those cultural, economic, societal and political points and positions which are against of the law and love of God. "Experience does not interpret itself; various modes of public discourse are required to discern the meaning of particular experiences," said M. Stackhouse many years ago.[6] The same author names four 'publics': the *authentic religious, political, academic* and *economic public* as the main areas of developing a consequential Public Theology. As a theological programme it needs the notions of *holiness, justice, truth,* and *creativity*, which are correlated with the public spheres mentioned.

The decisive point of any effective initiative of doing Public Theology well lies in the interpretation of faith for the Christians. The church not only has the ability to change the pervading world models of maleficence, but, simultaneously, it has to connect its members with God. What can and should be preached and taught to those who seek faithful living and thinking according to the most holy, and thus the most comprehensive, righteous, and enduring reality to which humans can point? This is not only a question of the past, asked by Stackhouse, but can be a real turning point in the present evil processes in creation.

Considering all this, how are we supposed to teach theology today? At the end of this paper I am going to mention briefly some examples from my practice.

6. Max L. Stackhouse, "Public theology and ethical judgment", *Theology Today*, 54 (2), 1997, p. 166.

How to Teach Theology Today? – Some Practical Examples

Realizing the importance of the practical side of public theology, it is worth mentioning some examples of dealing with public theological issues in the arena of theological studies. According to my experience, the public theology skills of the students can be improved by a combination of giving exercises and introducing concrete models of co-operation among the actors of beneficial social (as well as political, economic and ecological) activities. That is why I regularly invite notable actors of significant NGOs to our theology courses, where students can get authentic, expert and committed answers to their questions. This way they have the chance to start developing a viable systematic response of their own. After a conversation with an NGO leader, during the following class, the students discuss the theological inspiration, impulses and vision they received based on the information gained from the previous session. Further theological input can only be built on such well-founded and well-authenticated information. After carrying out a theological evaluation of this first phase I usually ask students to focus on the possibility of developing a comprehensive framework of reflections towards a kind of integrative theology. Although the contours of this framework can be rough, drawing it up develops the ability of systematic thinking, which is a *conditio sine qua non* of proper acting in global issues.

Another example of dealing with public theological issues in the theological academy is a translation course where significant selected texts are translated by ecumenical, interreligious and inter-institutional groups of students. This work can be done in co-operation with other universities, churches and organizations and its goal can be the publication of the translated texts in a book or on a webpage. Through these channels students and others can be provided with some essential and concentrated information about environmental, social, and other issues in a unique form. In addition, during the course, the students can make contacts in certain professional contexts, which can prove to be helpful for their future activities related to global issues.

A deep knowledge of the so-called *world problematique* and a deeply rooted living faith in Jesus Christ can serve together as sufficient ground for acting as Christians today. A humble and politically active Christian life needs information, experience, and endurance, but first and foremost it needs hope with regard to the created world of God. We can be at home at the university and have our homeland in the church at the same time. That is the motivation for engaging in academic theological work that pursues public theological issues in order to be acting as Christians in and for God's creation.

Bibliography

Batka, Lubomír. "Jedes Haus, das mit sich selbst uneins ist, kann nicht bestehen." Wo begegnen sich Theologie und Gesellschaft?, in: Jens Schröter and Sophie Kottsieper (ed.), *Die Rolle der Theologie in Universitaet, Gesellschaft und Kirche*, Leipzig: Evangelische Verlagsanstalt, 2012, p. 94

Callicott, J. B. and R. Frodeman (ed.). *Encyclopedia of Environmental Ethics and Philosophy*. USA: McMillan Reference, 2009, "water" p. 393.

Dalferth, Ingolf. *Radikale Theologie*. Leipzig: Evangelische Verlagsanstalt, 2010.

Forrester, Duncan B. "The Scope of Public Theology", *Studies in Christian Ethics*, 17 (2), (2004): p. 6.

Stackhouse, Max L. "Public theology and ethical judgment", *Theology Today*, 54 (2), (1997): p. 166.

CHAPTER 7

The Christian University: An Oxymoron or a Community of Faith and Knowledge?[1]

Tibor Fabiny

"Some seek knowledge for the sake of knowledge: that is curiosity; others seek knowledge that they may themselves be known: that is vanity; but there are still others who seek knowledge in order to serve and edify others, and that is charity." – St. Bernard of Clairvaux

The paper has four sections. In 'Section I' I expose and problematize the idea of a Christian university by asking whether the term is an oxymoron and by giving a short historical perspective; in 'Section II' I approach the question from my personal Hungarian post-Communist context; in 'Section III' I discuss the role of vision in the conception of the Christian university; in 'Section IV' I conclude with the (perhaps utopian) vision of the Christian university as a vibrant, open-minded community of faith and the community of knowledge.

---

1. This is a work-in-progress, reflecting mainly the personal experience of the author. Its purpose is to raise and articulate issues based on this experience. A shorter version of the paper was read at the Langham International Conference in Berekfürdő, Hungary, on 11 May 2013. Responses and critiques are most appreciated.

The Problem: Is There a 'Christian University'?

Let us start our train of thought with a reflection on the nature and mission of a Christian university.

An Oxymoron?

At first sight the idea of a 'Christian university' might strike us as an oxymoron (i.e. a contradiction in terms) – Christian faith means commitment to a closed (declarative, assertive and dogmatic) set of values while a university is committed to curiosity, openness, questioning, scepticism and academic freedom. To put it bluntly: if it is Christian, it cannot be a university, if it is a university, it cannot be Christian. Of course, I exaggerate, but I am doing this in order to clarify the identity of a Christian university.

The church and the university represent two ways of thinking and perhaps even two kinds of languages which sometimes seem to be incompatible or irreconcilable. The language of faith is declarative, assertive and revelatory and this cannot be said of the language used at the university either by the sciences or the humanities. The language of science is accurate, exact, referential, denotative; the language of the humanities, especially that of literature, is ambiguous, non-referential, metaphorical, connotative.

Neither the language of science nor that of the humanities conforms to the language of the church which is ultimately authoritative. The church from the very beginning speaks with the voice of authority invested upon her by its Founder. The university refuses to acknowledge such an *apriori* authority; however, it recognizes *aposteriori* authority, (i.e. authority in retrospect when it has proved itself and has been approved by the community of knowledge).

True, there have always been committed Christian theologians who were able to live up to the requirements of this double citizenship: they were loyal members of their churches, sometimes even of high ecclesiastical rank, and at the same time fully acknowledged members of the academic communities. They were members both of the community of faith and the community of knowledge. Nevertheless, while this double citizenship may work smoothly at the level of the individual, I doubt it can function without conflicts within the structure of church-related institutions.

In order to understand the present situation let us give a short historical perspective.

A Short Historical Perspective

In the past centuries the churches have functioned also as educators. In the Middle Ages knowledge was disseminated by the Roman Catholic Church. However, it not only disseminated but monopolized and controlled knowledge. The *universitas* was usually founded by the *ecclesia* and thus it was subordinate to it.

This relationship was radically changed in the time of the Reformation. Luther's reform meant that the *universitas* severed itself from the *ecclesia*, (i.e. Wittenberg from Rome). The Roman Church was seen as a corrupt institution whose theological and spiritual inertia could only be redeemed by the university. The university has triumphed over the church. The church's prestige has diminished while the university's prestige has spectacularly increased.[2]

During the seventeenth and eighteenth centuries the Protestant churches, especially across the Atlantic, were keen on establishing colleges and universities. However, in the United States we see examples of gradual secularization of originally 'sectarian' institutions of higher education. Princeton, Harvard, Yale and Duke Universities were originally founded by the Presbyterian or Methodist churches. In the process of secularization there has been a shift of priority from the founding vision to autonomy of the subjects taught and thus Christian faith has become marginalized. While the well-known Jonathan Edwards was one of the first presidents of the College of New Jersey (founded in 1746, now Princeton University), when the Presbyterian church leaders found that their College had come under secular influence, they founded Princeton Theological Seminary in 1812 which has flourished as one of the best theological institutions in the United States ever since. In other cases as at Yale, Harvard or Duke, the Divinity School remained a faculty of the University. Thus, the university has

---

2. Cf. John Van Engen, "Christianity and the University: The Medieval and Reformation Legacies", in, Joel A. Carpenter and Kenneth W. Shipps, *Making Higher Education Christian: The History and Mission of Evangelical Colleges in America* (Grand Rapids: William B. Eerdmans and Christian University Press, Christian College, 1987). pp.19–37.

become an autonomous institution which could fulfil its mission without the church. The descendants were usually meant to 'respect' the intention of the founders but this slight gesture of verbal loyalty provided autonomy.

The process of secularization has been long seen as a necessary process, and a fruitful one, in the United States. The sciences and the humanities could develop without the ideological control of the church. The community of knowledge has triumphed over the community of faith.

Recently, however, there has emerged a voice that speaks of the negative effects of the marginalization or the loss of religion. First it was the American historian of religion, George M. Marsden, who alerted the public concerning the negative effects of secularization of originally church-founded institutions of higher education in his book *The Soul of American University: From Protestant Establishment to Established Nonbelief.*[3] In reviewing the book the Jesuit J. A. Appleyard begins his reflections saying that,

> . . . most of the colleges and universities founded in the U.S. before the 20th century had a strongly religious, usually Protestant Christian, character and that virtually all of these institutions have no significant religious identity today. The best known example is Harvard, founded 'for the provision of learned ministry', whose motto for three centuries was 'Christo et Ecclesiae', but scores of other institutions – including Yale, Princeton, Chicago, Stanford, Duke, Boston University, and even the publicly founded state universities such as Michigan and California – had a pronounced Christian character in the early years of their existence and abandoned it in the 20th century.[4]

Marsden notes that within this process of secularization theology became more liberal and religious sentiment was translated into commitment

---

3. George M. Marsden, *The Soul of American University: From Protestant Establishment to Established Nonbelief* (Oxford: Oxford University Press, 1996).

4. http://www.bc.edu/content/dam/files/offices/mission/pdf1/ra2.pdf. Last visited on 1 May 2013.

to patriotism and democracy; the concept of academic freedom was felt incompatible with dogmatic belief and by establishing 'departments of religion', religion itself became merely an object of scientific study, religious tests for faculty hiring were abandoned and the principle norm became exclusively academic excellence. Moreover, some major foundations, for example the Carnegie Endowment, were committed to funding only non-sectarian institutions. Appleyard expressed his hope that Catholic colleges can perhaps avoid the trap of this secularization-process.

Another robust critique of this secularizing process is James Tunsead Burtchaell's *The Dying of the Light: The Disengagement of Colleges and Universities from Their Christian Churches*.[5] Acknowledging the insights of Marsden and Burtchaell, Robert Benne in his book *Quality with Soul: How Six Premier Colleges and Universities Keep Faith in Their Religious Traditions* was able to uphold the examples of Calvin College (Christian Reformed Church), Wheaton College (Evangelical Tradition), Baylor University (Southern Baptist Convention), The University of Notre Dame (Roman Catholic Church), St Olaf College (Evangelical Lutheran Church in America) and Valparaiso University (The Lutheran Church – Missouri Synod).[6] Benne thoroughly studied the original mission statements (vision) and the present practice (ethos) of these colleges and universities which, while preserving academic excellence by successfully integrating faith and learning, were able to resist the pressure of culture to give up their Christian identity.

Ten years after the publication of Marsden's book, C. John Sommerville published his *The Decline of the Secular University* (Oxford University Press, 2006) in which he argued that though secularization had promised to be a liberating force for church-founded universities, it failed its mission because the trivialization of religion resulted in the loss of values, the sense of history, the idea of defining the human and so on. In his review of the book George Marsden explains why he recommends it as the best

---

5. James Tunstead Burtchaell, *The Dying of the Light: The Disengagement of Colleges and Universities from Their Christian Churches* (Grand Rapids: Eerdmans, 1998).
6. Robert Benne, *Quality with Soul: How Six Premier Colleges and Universities Keep Faith in Their Religious Traditions* (Grand Rapids: Eerdmans, 2001).

case he has seen "for why the dogged secularism of many universities is undermining the announced purposes of higher education".[7]

Of course, secularists in the United States did not share the views of Marsden, Burtchaell, Benne and Sommerville, nevertheless these books alerted the public opinion to the negative effects of trivialization of religion in the secularization of church-related universities.

However, the development in Eastern Europe, especially in Hungary, seems to be different, if not the reverse, mainly because of forty years of Communism.[8] Now I am going to contextualize the issue by sharing my own personal experience in Hungary.

Experience – From a Personal Perspective

A Personal Journey into Christian Higher Education

I was brought up the son of a Lutheran pastor (later a professor of Church History) in Communist Hungary. The Communists nationalized all church-related secondary schools of the Lutheran Church by the early 1950s so both my primary and secondary education took place in state-schools dominated by Marxist-atheist ideology. Being a 'pastor's kid' I was seen usually as a kind of curiosity in my classrooms; however, the negative discrimination of the early 1960s gradually and unnoticeably shifted into an attitude of 'respected alterity' by the mid 1970s.

The system silently tolerated that some teachers were discretely churchgoing people while, of course, not allowing them to articulate their faith before their pupils. I also had the good fortune of having been surrounded by some teachers of good will who gently tried to detain me from applying to study at a Faculty of Humanities. They said it was not really a good choice for a 'p-kid' to study at the Faculty of Humanities, since the humanities were ideologically loaded disciplines and therefore

---

7. http://www.oup.com/us/catalog/general/subject/ReligionTheology/American/?view=us a&ci=9780195306958. Last visited on 1 May 2013.

8. Cf. Perry L. Glanzer, "The Death and Resurrection of Protestant Higher Education in Europe: A Case Study" in *The International Handbook of Protestant Education* (pp. 195–224), eds. William Jeynes and David Robinson (New York: Springer Press, 2012).

it was especially difficult for ideologically non-friendly applicants like me to get in. They wanted to be sure that somebody with an ecclesiastical pedigree would not undermine or infect the solid atheistic educational system of the regime.

Nevertheless I applied to study my favourite subject, English. Because I chose Library Science as a second subject I was probably seen more as a future researcher than a teacher. I was accepted to study at the Faculty of Humanities in 1973. To many people this seemed to be almost a miracle in Communist Hungary. And an even greater surprise was when seven years later, after my graduation in 1980, I was invited to be an assistant Lecturer of English Literature at the Faculty of Humanities at József Attila University of Szeged. It was still Communist but the climate was already different: the anti-establishment, critical intellectual elite of the Faculty of Szeged University began to look favourably at dissident thinkers and they sought and found support in me in defying the dull ideological clichés of the, by then, more and more irrelevant and impotent Marxism.

And indeed: teaching Shakespeare in the 1980s offered a unique opportunity for me to silently challenge and subvert totalitarian ideology. Shakespeare's plays (*Hamlet, Richard III, As You Like It, Macbeth* or *The Tempest*) were about 'time out of joint' and in most of them Machiavellian usurpers usually dismissed the lawful rulers and this created a world upside down, the beginning of tragedy. In these worlds the legitimate ones were banished or marginalized and the illegitimate ones were wicked and perverted usurpers. Was it not the case after 1956 in János Kádár's corrupt and unlawful regime? Within the rubrics of academic freedom I taught Shakespeare but the students' minds were opened to recognize and see parallels between the issue of the plays and the contemporary political situation.

Moreover, I could witness to my Christian faith indirectly, by teaching English literature (medieval moralities as *Everyman*, poetry of Donne, Milton, Eliot, the novels of Bunyan, etc.), works that were permeated by Christianity, which I selected for classroom discussions. And three years before the fall of the iron curtain I even developed a course on the English Bible as part of the "Intellectual Background of English Literature".

Having taught for more than a decade at the University of Szeged I was invited to serve as a scholar-in-residence at Roanoke College, Virginia. It was a Liberal Arts College founded by the Lutheran Church in the mid-nineteenth century.[9] It was my first experience to teach at a church-related college. I saw that a minority of the faculty wanted to be faithful to the College's Lutheran heritage while a majority tried to sever that link as much as possible following the example of the secularization of the great American universities mentioned earlier.

I came to see that for committed Christians this double loyalty (loyalty to the church and loyalty to the academy) was indeed a heavy burden. I remember at Roanoke an eye-opening lecture of my colleague Dr Ned Wisnefsky on the ethos of the Lutheran College which is both a community of faith and a community of knowledge[10] to which I shall return in Section 3. Let it suffice here to say that the faith-community is smaller but it articulates and defends the institution's original religious vision. The academic community is larger and several of their members are ideology-free, (i.e. not Christian and especially not Lutheran) but they necessarily make compromises for a *modus vivendi*.

The semester I spent at Roanoke College turned out to be an excellent experiment for me to investigate the relationship between church and academia. This prepared me for my return to Hungary (1993) when I was invited to organize and chair the English Department at the newly established Pázmány Péter Catholic University. At the same time, I became the director of the Centre for Hermeneutical Research, an ecumenical foundation hosted by Károli Gáspár University of the Reformed Church in Hungary.

The problems I had to face were familiar from my Roanoke College experience. Double loyalty: to the church and Christian values on the one hand and to neutral, purely academic values on the other hand. (Here

---

9. See Robert Benne, "A College Recovers its Christian Identity" http://www.religion-online.org/showarticle.asp?title=2095. Originally published in *The Christian Century*, 18–25 April, 2001, pp. 12–15.

10. Ned Wisnefske, "The Lutheran College: A Community of Learning, a Community of Faith." in *Papers and Proceedings of the 79th Annual Meeting, Lutheran Educational Conference of North America*, 7–10 February 1993, pp. 6–13.

my case was even more complicated as I was a Lutheran among Roman Catholics.) As the Head of Department I was faced with the dilemma whether to hire committed Christians with perhaps lower academic credentials or academically excellent ones with no, or hardly any, Christian commitment. Of course, one always wants to find the proper balance, but my priorities were in academic excellence.

After a decade or so I was invited to be in charge of the English Department at the Károli Gáspár University of the Reformed Church in Hungary. Now, as a Lutheran I am at least among Protestants but still not a member of the church that runs this institution. And I have been faced with the same dilemma again. Several non-Christian faculty are associated with these new church-related institutions on the basis of a mutual practical compromise: they simply need jobs and the church-related university needs professional expertise.

Issues and Dilemmas in the Experience of Christian Higher Education

My dilemma is: what should be the expectations of these institutions towards these colleagues with regards to Christian values? How to avoid the danger of ideological sycophancy, or, on the other hand, the hidden agenda of subverting Christian values? Are these the only dangers lurking in our midst?

As for the present, I perceive three possible dangers in the existence and structure of our Christian universities: a) ideological sycophancy; b) the hidden agenda of intellectual subversion of Christian values; and c) the conversion of religious sentiments, or the lack of them, into political ones.

Ideological Sycophancy

By ideological sycophancy I mean the detestable attitude of some colleagues who, for promoting themselves and securing their own position within an ecclesiastical institution, pretend to be Christian or at least conform to the values of a Christian or Protestant university without being able to show some evidence or sign of their commitment. Some of them had usually good positions in Communist institutions and learned there how to be time-servers and now, as the political climate changed, they turn their coats and instead of the language of Communist ideology they choose to flatter their superiors in Christian phraseology in their newly adopted loyalty. Sycophancy is detestable, and hypocrisy, in my view, is the greatest enemy of Christian faith.

Intellectual Subversion

On the other hand, a danger of a different kind is also lurking around the fragile foundations of a Christian university. I vividly remember those years when I could silently challenge Communist ideology with the teaching of Shakespeare. What if some of my colleagues, like me thirty years ago, have also a hidden agenda, and, in the rubrics of academic freedom, use their professional expertise to undermine classical Christian values? Should, for example, gay and lesbian literature and criticism be taught at a Christian university? Should I respect the academic freedom of colleagues wishing to teach subjects like this, or, should I occasionally emerge in the unpopular dress of a dogmatic watchdog? No, being a dogmatic watchdog is definitely not the way one should act in civilized circumstances but what if one perceives that God's Kingdom is regressing rather than progressing in our classrooms?

Politicizing of Religious Sentiments

In Hungary after the political changes of 1990 not only were two religiously affiliated universities founded but hundreds of primary and secondary schools were re-affiliated with the mainline churches. The churches frequently loudly claimed that the state should give back their schools and institutions that they had nationalized between 1948 and 1952. This seems to be a fair argument on the surface but in reality it fails to notice that in the 1990s the churches were not what they were forty years before. It fails to notice that not only were the state institutes corrupted and ruined with Communist ideology, but with the help of secret agents within the churches (frequently bishops or professors), the churches as moral bodies were even more wounded.[11] Church leaders in the early 1990s were haunted by their

---

11. One should, of course, differentiate between agents who nominally accepted this task perhaps naively hoping that by this they could somehow serve the interest of their churches, and the ones who cynically betrayed their fellow Christians. (See my essay "The

own dark past and the process of purification has not been accomplished even until now.

Society has been naive and manipulated when they expected a moral breakthrough from the religious institutions. It happened quite frequently that the leadership of the schools was not changed when the churches took over these institutions. Old leaders, once loyal to the Communist party, frequently even party members, now suddenly turned around and adopted a rhetoric of loyalty to their church leaders. Faith, unlike political sentiments, does not inflame the younger generation. My thesis is that religiously affiliated schools, because of the lack of authentic faith and the institutional communication of it, easily could become prey of radical, in most cases right wing, political sentiments.

It is no wonder that students coming to a Christian university from such schools brought along these political sentiments with them. For a certain period they even enjoyed the support of the highly talented and charismatic Bishop, the founder of Károli Gáspár University who, for all his good will, associated himself with the ideology of a nationalistic, right-wing party. When the Bishop died in February 2013 it was announced on his mourning card that he was the 'Bishop of the Hungarians' and not just the Bishop of the Reformed Church in Hungary. If such neo-pagan heresy haunts the church, it is natural that the vacuum of Christian faith can easily be filled by radical, right-wing political sentiments.

The Vision – A Community of Faith and a Community of Knowledge

According Bob Benne there are three components of the Christian tradition that are publicly relevant for Christian colleges and universities: its vision, its ethos (practice) and the people who "understand and articulate the Christian vision and embody the ethos of that particular tradition".[12] I

Drama of Reconciliation in the Post-Communist Hungarian Church" in, Robert Schreiter and Knud Jørgensen, eds., *Mission As Ministry of Reconciliation* (Oxford Centre of Mission Studies, 2013), pp. 231–238).

12. Benne, *Quality,* p. 8.

shall deal with the first aspect at more length and briefly summarize the other two by applying them to the personal context I have been discussing so far.

Vision

A Christian university is born out of a theological vision. Though at the end of my paper I shall argue for the relevance of a Christian rather than of a denominational identity, it must be acknowledged that a theological vision is usually the result of a particular theological interpretation. I would like to offer three such theological interpretations: the Roman Catholic, the Reformed and the Lutheran. It seems useful to relate these interpretations to three of the five models offered by the H. R. Niebuhr's now classic *Christ and Culture* (Harper Torchbooks, 1951).[13]

The Roman Catholic vision, characterized by unity and integrity, corresponds to the model of 'Christ above culture'. According to this vision Christ appears "as a supernatural fulfilment of the aspirations of culture, in the same way that grace is seen as perfecting nature and theology as perfecting philosophy . . . All learning pointed, with the assistance of revelation and grace, toward the supernatural source of the world and reason and toward the supernatural end of humanity, which is the contemplation of God."[14]

A Christian university, as John Paul II declared in his Apostolic Constitution on Catholic universities, is born out of the 'heart of the church' – '*Ex Corde Ecclesiae*' (1990). It explicitly said that,

> A Catholic University's privileged task is to unite existentially
> by intellectual effort two orders of reality that too frequently
> tend to be placed in opposition as though they were

---

13. Here I shall rely on the analysis of an excellent article by Mark U. Edwards, Jr. "Christian Colleges: A Dying Light or a New Refraction?", in, *Christian Century*, 21–28 April 1999, pp. 459–463. Available also on the internet: http://www.religion-online.org/ showarticle.asp?title=547. I am quoting the internet source.

14. Edwards, "Christian Colleges".

antithetical: the search for truth, and the certainty of already knowing the fount of truth.[15]

This sentence hits the nail on the head as it recognizes that both the community of faith and the community of knowledge are concerned with the question of truth. The former is committed to the search for truth and the latter is committed to the "certainty of the fount of truth". Accordingly, the vision of a Christian (or Catholic) university is to 'unite' these two orders of reality. So the tension I was speaking of in Section I is not to be removed but it has to be made effective and creative.

The Reformed theological vision corresponds to the model of "Christ the Transformer of Culture". According to this vision, everything on earth and in human existence belongs to, and is therefore ruled by, Christ. A leading figure of the Reformed vision of education was the Dutch Abraham Kuyper (1837–1920), a theologian, university founder and politician. Kuyperian Calvinists lay the emphasis on the integration of faith (revelation) and learning (culture). Followers of Christ are, therefore, invited to transform this world. Christian philosophers, politicians, and artists, it is believed, can make this world better. No wonder therefore, that it has been a frequent practice, both globally and also in Hungary, that Reformed clergy who began their careers as congregational pastors eventually turned politicians in their (originally theological) hope that once they were in the arena of the public square, they would make it better. The Kuyperian theology has been embraced by, for example, Calvin College, Michigan, and this vision is ultimately the basis of George Marsden's already quoted magisterial book *The Soul of the University* in which he regrets the loss of Christian values of the once church-related colleges and universities and the marginalization of 'Christian scholarship'.[16]

The Lutheran Vision, argues the Reformation historian and the Lutheran St Olaf's College ex-President Mark U. Edwards, is characterized by the Niebuhrian – ultimately Lutheran – model of "Christ and Culture

---

15. http://www.vatican.va/holy_father/john_paul_ii/apost_constitutions/documents/hf_jp-ii_apc_15081990_ex-corde-ecclesiae_en.html last visited on 1 May 2013.
16. George Marsden, *The Outrageous Idea of Christian Scholarship.* (Oxford University Press, 1997).

in Paradox". Luther made a distinction between the two kingdoms: the sacred and the secular; the world of Christ and the world of culture. Though both realms are ruled and governed by God, it is done in different ways. Luther said that it is the art of making distinctions that defines a theologian. He recognized the tension and the paradox between the worlds and deliberately avoided creating any 'synthesis' between them. Education definitely belongs to the secular realm and, therefore, suggests Edwards, we should not lament the disappearance of 'Christian scholarship'. For Edwards, both the Catholic and the Reformed visions or models opine for an ideal, normative view of what Christian education 'should be' and they see every deviation from this ideal regrettable. Unlike them, the Lutheran Edwards sees the present situation not necessarily as the time of the 'dying light' but, rather of a 'new refraction'. His conclusion is worth quoting:

> We need to remember that the faithfulness of the church and of the church's institutions, including colleges, depends ultimately not on what we do for ourselves but what the Holy Spirit does for us. God has shown throughout the centuries, in the Bible stories and in church history, that God can accomplish God's purposes despite all the human weaknesses and foolishness that stand in the way. A sense of humility and, yes, an accompanying sense of humour are not out of place. We need to be able to laugh at our pretensions and shortcomings. And God can be trusted to preserve the colleges of the church in the form and way that God wills.[17]

In fact, a very similar conclusion was drawn by a Valparasio Lutheran theologian Mark R. Schwen. Though at first, evoking the ideas of the nineteenth century Catholic Cardinal John Henry Newman (1801–1890) and his classic *The Idea of the University* (1854), Schwen eloquently argued for the principles of 'unity', 'universality' and 'integrity' (loosely coinciding with the Trinitarian framework of creation, redemption and sanctification). However, towards the end of his essay, he came to argue that the "Christian

---

17. Edwards, "Christian Colleges".

university is the one that is most at odds with Newman".[18] With the philosopher Charles Taylor, Schwen believed that "modern culture, in breaking with the structures and beliefs of Christendom, also carried certain facets of Christian life further than they ever were taken, or could have been taken, within Christendom."[19] Similarly to Mark U. Edwards Jr, Schwen also proposed "to be more sanguine about the present state of Christianity and higher education". This Lutheran *hilaritas* is the underlying tone of the representative views of the third model.

> The Christian university can truly be itself only in a context of institutional pluralism, as one of several models, perhaps even a model on the margins, of university education. Christianity functions most truly and most effectively when it is disenthralled. And in this regard the life of the ideal Christian university is like unto the life of the individual Christian. Insofar as Christians relax their grip upon the reins of earthly dominion and contract the scope of their temporal ambitions, they so far increase the range of their spiritual influence and so the more steadily secure their hold upon eternity. This too should be a teaching of a Christian university.[20]

Therefore, the three versions of a Christian vision of university can be summarized by the following three statements: the Catholic vision encourages an overarching conversation between a secular and a robust theological perspective; the Calvinist vision seeks to transform secular culture completely; the Lutheran vision is happy to accept a more modest role for the Christian voice in the cacophony of the pluralistic community of a university. Though I recognize the feasibility of all the three visions, my conclusion in this paper is closest to the Lutheran one.

---

18. Mark R. Schwen, "A Christian University: Defining the Difference", in, *First Things* 93, May 1999, pp. 25–31. Also available on the internet: http://www.firstthings.com/article/2007/01/a-christian-universitydefining-the-difference-17. I quote the internet version.

19. Schwen, "A Christian University: Defining the Difference".

20. Ibid.

Ethos

Ethos is concerned with what is being done to achieve the identity of a Christian university. What are the characteristic contents of Christian higher education? Schwein in the above mentioned article said that in a Christian institute of higher education there should be a department of theology, an active chapel ministry, a faculty "that carry in and among themselves the DNA of the school",[21] and a curriculum including courses that articulate the vision.

People: A Community of Faith and a Community of Knowledge

Among Schwein's criteria the third one is indeed problematic – that faculty should "carry in and among themselves the DNA of the school". At some American colleges (e.g. at Calvin College) where faculty are hired only if they are members of the sponsoring church and sign a statement that they would be committed to integrate faith and learning in their teaching, the Schwein-criterion of the 'DNA' might work.

However, for several church-related Christian schools (including the 20-year-old Hungarian Pázmány Péter Catholic and Károli Gáspár Reformed Universities) this model would not work, partly because these institutions are also sponsored by the state, and because there are only a few faculty that come from the universities' respective church traditions. As suggested earlier, the situation is based on a compromise: the church-related universities need enough expertise (most professors have to be hired outside of their respective religious traditions) and professional experts with their PhDs are happy to be offered a job that they are qualified for. Thus within a Christian university it is usually a minority that belongs to the faith-community, the majority is only a member of the community of learning. A Christian university is, using the term of St Augustine, is a *corpux mixtum* at vengeance!

How can, or should, a Christian university which is both a community of faith and a community of knowledge, reconcile its inherent tension?

---

21. Ibid.

How far do these two communities overlap with each other? Or are they the only communities at Christian universities?

My focus is now on the University of the Reformed Church in Hungary. We have had leaders – some of them better than others – new ideas and new structures have been introduced, some other structures have suddenly disappeared. We have wonderful colleagues and wonderful students. Most of us are happy within our walls, but unfortunately rarely, or hardly ever, do we stop to reflect on the mission (vision, ethos, people) of our church-affiliated university. A good innovation was the introduction of the so-called biannual 'training weeks' (short-term mandatory classes of great variety for students and leadership development workshops with entertaining programmes for faculty) at Károli University, but there has not been enough reflection on their effects.

How far can the community of faith define the profile of a Christian institution of higher education? Can the community of faith affect the community of knowledge? Ned Wisnefsky in his above-mentioned article offered an answer to this question:

> There are three principal ways in which a community of faith can affect a community of learning within Lutheran Colleges: by establishing a religious context within which learning takes place; by helping set the goal of learning; by influencing the content of what is learned.[22]

It is significant that Wisnefsky's focus is not only on the structure of such an institution or on the faculty, but on the students for whom he insists on defining the context, the goal and the content of learning.

---

22. Wisnefsky, "The Lutheran College". p. 6.

Conclusion: A (Perhaps Utopian?) Vision of a Vibrant, Open-minded, Faith-oriented Community

In conclusion, I am suggesting the university should really be concerned with defining its Reformed/Protestant/Christian identity. How far should this identity be manifested in the personal commitment of faculty and the formation of the curriculum?

At the Catholic University, the requirement was that at least 50 per cent of the faculty should be Roman Catholic and the rest could be anything. Frankly, I felt somewhat uncomfortable that as a Lutheran Christian, I found myself in the group of atheists, agnostics, (i.e. 'the anything').

In my view the community of faith, especially in the age of ecumenism, should have more of a Christian rather than a rigid denominational identity however different theological interpretations (models) determined the visions of the founding fathers. Ultimately, a Christian vision, including the input of Orthodox, Roman Catholics, Lutherans, Calvinists, and Evangelical believers should be able to contribute to the making of the identity of a Christian university, whether Roman Catholic or Reformed.

The larger community of knowledge should respect the identity-forming efforts of the community of faith while the community of faith should respect academic excellence.

The third and so far undiscussed community is that of the administration. They interfere with both the community of faith and the community of knowledge. The professional aspect should be emphasized here too – you do not have to necessarily be a committed Christian to be a good manager. However, it is good to know that there are some excellent Christian managers too!

By making these borders visible, non-believing faculty members could honestly pursue their professional and educational efforts without being forced to hypocrisy or sycophancy. Such openness would be mutually productive. A vivid and honest discussion of faith-issues would make a Christian university distinct from any other secular universities where faith-issues are either taboo or non-existent. Yes, we can rejoice when some of our faculty, though coming from an atheistic or agnostic background, are open to, sometimes even keen on, accepting the values of the community of faith. I have first-hand personal experience of colleagues who, during their tenure, were baptized and became very active members of their local churches. True, at a Christian university, the direction of this process might also work the other way. In a secularized world, whether we like it or not, faith can also diminish and formerly committed Christians might start talking about their newly adopted 'post-Christian' views.

Whatever the situation is, an open-minded church-related university should promote vibrant and honest discussion of faith-issues. How fruitful it would be to initiate 'faith and learning' discussions for both faculty and students or to organize 'questions of faith' series for members of both communities of learning and communities of faith!

This also means that the Christian university should not close its door to evangelization either of the students or of the faculty. The Christian faith, after all, is a missionary faith. However, the freedom of conscience, again an old Protestant value, of every individual within our walls should be highly respected. The missionary faith of a Christian university, though a university cannot and should not take over the task of the church, could also be articulated, avoiding, of course, aggressive proselytization. Ultimately, a Christian university, with the help of its church, could always express a readiness in offering, if there is willingness to take it, the treasure of its founding parent, the *thesaurus ecclesiae*, the gospel.

Bibliography

Appleyard, J. A. "The Secularization of the Modern American University". *Conversations*, 10 (1996): 31-33. Available through http://www.bc.edu/content/dam/files/offices/mission/pdf1/ra2.pdf (Accessed on 1 May 2013).

Benne, Robert. *Quality with Soul: How Six Premier Colleges and Universities Keep Faith in Their Religious Traditions*. Grand Rapids: Eerdmans, 2001.

———. "A College Recovers its Christian Identity", *The Christian Century*, (18–25 April 2001): 12–15. Also available on http://www.religion-online.org/showarticle.asp?title=2095.

Burtchaell, James Tunstead. *The Dying of the Light: The Disengagement of Colleges and Universities from Their Christian Churches*. Grand Rapids: Eerdmans, 1998.

Edwards, Mark U., Jr. "Christian Colleges: A Dying Light or a New Refraction?", *Christian Century*, (21–28 April 1999): 459–463. Also Available on http://www.religion-online.org/showarticle.asp?title=547.

Engen, John van. "Christianity and the University: The Medieval and Reformation Legacies", in: Joel A. Carpenter and Kenneth W. Shipps, *Making Higher Education Christian: The History and Mission of Evangelical Colleges in America*. Grand Rapids, William B. Eerdmans and Christian University Press, Christian College, 1987, pp.19–37.

Fabiny, Tibor. "The Drama of Reconciliation in the Post-Communist Hungarian Church" in: Robert Schreiter and Knud Jørgensen, eds. *Mission As Ministry of Reconciliation*. Oxford: Oxford Centre of Mission Studies, 2013, pp. 231–238.

Glanzer, Perry L. "The Death and Resurrection of Protestant Higher Education in Europe: A Case Study" in: William Jeynes and David Robinson (eds) *The International Handbook of Protestant Education*. New York: Springer Press, 2012, pp. 195–224.

John Paul II. "Apostolic Constitution on Catholic Universities. Ex corde Ecclesiae", August 15, 1990. Available through http://www.vatican.va/holy_father/john_paul_ii/apost_constitutions/documents/hf_jp-ii_apc_15081990_ex-corde-ecclesiae_en.html (Accessed on 1 May 2013).

Marsden, George. *The Soul of American University: From Protestant Establishment to Established Nonbelief.* Oxford: Oxford University Press, 1996.

———. *The Outrageous Idea of Christian Scholarship*. Oxford: Oxford University Press, 1997.

———. Review of "The Decline of the Secular University" by C. John Sommerville. Available through http://www.oup.com/us/catalog/general/subject/ReligionTheology/American/?view=usa&ci=9780195306958. (Accessed on 1 May 2013).

Schwen, Mark R., "A Christian University: Defining the Difference", *First Things* 93, (May 1999): 25–31. Also available on http://www.firstthings.com/article/2007/01/a-christian-universitydefining-the-difference-17.

Wisnefske, Ned. "The Lutheran College: A Community of Learning, a Community of Faith". in *Papers and Proceedings of the 79th Annual Meeting, Lutheran Educational Conference of North America*, 7–10 February 1993, pp. 6–13.

CHAPTER 8

Faith and Learning: Re-visiting the Idea of Christian University

Corneliu Constantineanu

If the very idea and purpose of university is being debated nowadays, it is even more so with our talk about a religious-based education, in particular a 'Christian university' – a truth expressed clearly by George Marsden who entitled one of his significant books, *The Outrageous Idea of Christian Scholarship.*[1] However, the fact of the matter is that the end of the twentieth century and the beginning of the twenty-first marked a revitalization of religious higher education, and this, I am sure, is a surprise for many. But this is exactly the conclusion reached by research done through Lilly Endowment's Initiative on Religion and Higher Education, which highlights that, "there is today more discussion about the role of religion in the academy than at any time in the past 40 years and more commitment to the project of Christian higher education than there was just ten years ago."[2] If that is the case, it is worth re-visiting the idea of the Christian university and to explore what would be its distinctive contribution, if any, to the larger field of university education. And this is the purpose of this paper. I begin with a reference to the surprising 'return' of religion in the

---

1. George Marsden, *The Outrageous Idea of Christian Scholarship* (Oxford, New York: Oxford University Press, 1998).

2. Kathleen A. Mahoney et al, *Revitalizing Religion in the Academy* (Chesntnut Hill: Boston College Press, 2000), p. 13.

social arena and then address the integration of faith and learning pointing out several models for integration. Finally, I will present some distinctive elements of a Christian university project.

The Re-emergence of Religion in the Social Arena

There is an obvious and somewhat surprising reality in the public square: religion has become a major factor in the social and political arena.[3] If the end of the nineteenth and beginning of the twentieth century were dominated by a view of general scepticism regarding the role and future place of religion on the social arena,[4] the end of the twentieth and beginning of the twenty-first century mark a spectacular and somewhat unexpected return of the religious phenomenon as an important factor in the public sphere. In recent decades the role of religion has been seen as particularly influential as a potential factor for social stability/ instability and as the motivation for individual conduct, indeed as an 'absolute necessity for democracy'.[5] The results of a decade of empirical studies conducted by Emory University throughout the world on religious sources and dimensions of human rights and democracy have confirmed that religion is a vital dimension of any democracy, as it offers the highest framework of reference and values, and gives content and coherence to the structure of human communities and cultures.[6] More specifically the study reveals that,

---

3. See, for example, Graham Ward and Michael Hoelzl (eds.), *The New Visibility of Religion: Studies in Religion and Cultural Hermeneutics* (London, New York: Continuum, 2008).

4. We could only mention here the influence of Feuerbach, followed by that of the three 'masters of suspicion', Marx, Nietzsche, and Freud who had an enormous 'contribution' to the attempt to limit the significance of the religious phenomenon and, indeed, to eradicate it completely as a dimension of human existence.

5. Christoph Von Schönborn, *Oamenii, Biserica, Tara. Crestinismul ca provocare sociala* (Bucharest: Anastasia, 2000), p. 87.

6. The findings of these projects were published in various journal publications and in a two-volume work entitled *Religious Human Rights in Global Perspective* (The Hague and London: Martinus Nijoff, 1996).

Religion is an ineradicable condition of human persons and communities. Religion invariably provides universal sources and scales of values by which many persons and communities govern and measure themselves. Religion invariably provides the sources and scales of dignity and responsibility, shame and respect, restitution and reconciliation that democracy and human rights need to survive and to flourish. Religions must thus be seen as indispensable allies in the modern struggle for human rights and democratization. Their faith and works, their symbols and structures, must be adduced to give meaning and measure to the abstract claims of democratic and human rights norms.[7]

The religious factor cannot thus be ignored or dismissed since it plays a major role in the fabric of human society. In the words of sociologist Peter Berger, religion represents 'the sacred canopy', 'the symbolic universe' within which people live and which helps integrate the various aspects of life, thus providing a comprehensive understanding of reality and the meaning of life.[8] That is why one's faith and one's God represent for most religious people the ultimate reality to which they give total allegiance. Thus, faith and/or God for many people still remains the ultimate point of reference for one's life and no amount of external impositions or legislation will be able to shape fundamentally the worldview of a believer as much as his/her faith does.

The findings of the project, however, revealed a paradox regarding the actual contribution of religious groups. They have shown that high religiosity among people is not directly proportional with concrete implications on the social, cultural, political and economic realities of the country. There is clearly a lack of correlation between the predominant

---

7. John Witte Jr., "Introduction: Pluralism, Proselytism, and Nationalism in Eastern Europe", in *Journal of Ecumenical Studies* XXVI (1999), p. 1.

8. See particularly Peter L. Berger, *The Sacred Canopy: Elements of Sociological Theory of Religion* (New York: Doubleday, 1969); Peter Berger and T. Luckman, *The Social Construction of Reality: A Treatise in the Sociology of Knowledge* (New York: Doubleday, 1967); Peter Berger, ed., *The Desecularisation of the World* (Grand Rapids: Eerdmans, 2000).

religiosity and the actual practice of life. Similar conclusions are confirmed by surveys conducted in recent years on the religious attitudes in Western Europe and in Central and Eastern Europe. They have found that while in Western Europe on average three in four people are associated with a particular religion, in Eastern Europe over 80 per cent of people identified themselves as religious.[9] Romania ranks among the highest in Europe in religious adherence, with an astonishing 99.96 per cent of the population indicating they belong to a religious group. However, the implications of this high religiosity for the everyday life of people and its effect on the concrete social, cultural, political and economic realities of the country reveal a disturbing and contradictory reality. Romania, the country with the highest ranking of religiosity in Europe, is also among the leading countries in terms of corruption, poverty and lack of trust.[10] This discrepancy, to be sure, does not invalidate the thesis that religion has a potential for being a positive factor for social, economic, and political change. It shows, however, at least two things: first, that the religious 'potential' is not automatically translatable into the social realities; and, second, that it is not just any kind of religiosity that could contribute effectively to human flourishing and wellbeing. Thus, for an effective and beneficial practice of religion and in order for its potential to bring about hope, compassion, reconciliation, and social healing, it is mandatory to find resources within our own religious texts and traditions and explicate them in ways that are relevant to the concrete social and political realities of the communities. We need to explore and articulate clearly and forcefully those aspects of our faith that teach us how to love our neighbours and our enemies, how to relate to 'the other', how to live together with our deepest differences. We need to emphasize those teachings that promote human dignity, justice, love, forgiveness, peace and

---

9. *GfK Custom Research Worldwide* on behalf of Wall Street Journal Europe, Nuremberg/ Frankfurt, 10 December 2004.

10. Silviu Rogobete, "Between Fundamentalism and Secularization: the Place and the Role of Religion in Post-Communist Orthodox Romania," in *Religion and Democracy in Moldova*. Edited by S. Devetak, O. Sirbu and S. Rogobete (Maribor/ Chisinau: ISCOMET/ASER, 2005), pp. 105–110. See also Tom Gallagher's impressive and detailed analysis of the complex causes and factors which undermined the development of a stable, independent, and autonomous democracy in Romania, *Theft of a Nation: Romania Since Communism* (London: C. Hearst & Co, 2004).

reconciliation. There is thus a need to uncover and nurture a religiosity that will be beneficial and conducive to human flourishing, a religiosity that will best enable us to live authentically with our fellow human beings. If we work within this framework of reference regarding faith, then it is logical to discuss and explore the issue of education from a religious perspective.

The Search for Integration

The contemporary mode in education in our society is very fragmented. The compartmentalization of knowledge, while it has had some advantages and has led to significant and wonderful discoveries, has also led to a fragmentation of our lives in different compartments: scientific, religious, social, etc. However, the reality within which we live is complex, inter-connected and inter-related and one cannot simply separate and segregate the pieces. We have to understand and cope with life as a whole, in all its diversity and complexity.

There is nowadays a great cry for integration, for a meaningful way of life in which one can make sense of and integrate all dimensions of life. We are witnessing also a constant preoccupation among Christian intellectuals and scholars to integrate faith within everyday realities of life in society. Young people especially, but not solely, raise serious and urgent questions: How is my faith connected with all other dimensions of life? Is faith just private or has it also to do with the public domain? Is there a place for Christian witness in a secular environment, and if yes, how is that witness to be displayed with integrity in such a context? What does it mean to be an authentic Christian in a secular and pluralist context?

From a Christian perspective, the fundamental drive for this kind of whole-life integration has its basis in the reality of the lordship of Christ over all creation, in all matters private and public. This is excellently illustrated in the life and writings of Abraham Kuyper (1837–1920), a Dutch Reformed theologian, journalist, university founder and statesman. In his inaugural speech ('Sphere Sovereignty') at the opening of Free University which he founded in 1880, Kuyper expresses Christ's lordship over all things in remarkable and unforgettable words: "Oh, no single piece of our mental world is to be hermetically sealed off from the rest, and there is not a square inch in the whole domain of our human existence over which Christ, who is Sovereign over all, does not cry: 'Mine!'"[11] Such a holistic perspective is vital for Christian education and we have to fully understand and relate it to the complex, dynamic and intrinsic relationships between the various dimensions of life. There is thus an urgent need in the contemporary world to find ways to relate faith to all aspects of life.

The Tension Requiring the Integration of Faith and Learning: Models of Integration[12]

When we talk specifically about faith and learning, there are other causes for a search for integration. Particularly, this is given by the seeming tension between aspects of faith and aspects of academic inquiry. There are several developments in various fields of knowledge which seem to be in tension with some aspects of faith. We can give two brief examples of tension from the field of psychology. First, there is the deterministic understanding of the person, according to which the life of a human being is totally determined by genetics and the environment; this seems to come in contradiction with a biblical and Christian theological view in which human beings have creativity and freedom as well as responsibility. Second, there is a psychological understanding and view of the goodness of a human being (hindered just by his own internal inhibitions and the external bad influences – but out of which the person can free herself), which seems incompatible with the biblical and Christian emphasis on influence and captivity of sin.

Many Christian academics have to live with such tensions. As Christians *and* scientists, they are not ready to give up either of the two and, therefore, they look for ways to understand the two dimensions of existence and

---

11. James D. Bratt, ed., *Abraham Kuyper: A Centennial Reader* (Grand Rapids: Eerdmans, 1998), p. 488.

12. In the discussion of this section I follow the argument of Nicholas Wolterstorff, "The Integration of faith and learning: the very idea", in his *Educating for Shalom: Essays on Christian Higher Education* (Grand Rapids: Eerdmans, 2004), pp. 36–45.

integrate the two aspects – thus, relieving the tension in a suitable manner. This very existential tension determines the search for integration of faith and learning.

In order to release the tension that is perceived between faith and academy, people have used several strategies and models for integration. Nicholas Wolterstorff points out three such ways of integration: *harmonization, compatibilism,* and *delimitation.* In the harmonizing model, in order to release the tension we decide to give up on some aspects of Christian faith: "we revise our understanding of the faith so as to harmonize it with our scientific convictions."[13] In this case it is assumed that there is a real conflict, and that something must go – in this scenario what goes are aspects of Christian faith. An immediate alternative would be to assume that the tension is not a real conflict and so one needs to give up nothing. No need for revision of either faith or science. This way of integration is called *compatibilism*: "Two truths, mysterious that they should both be true; but so it is. When doing science we speak as scientists; when engaged in religious activities we speak as religious people. These are simply two languages, each with its own vocabulary, speaking about one complex reality; difficulty arises only if we try to mingle the languages."[14] But this strategy of integration may not be the best one as it seems more difficult to live with 'mysteries'.

The third way of attempting to solve the tension is the so-called *delimitation.* Those who follow this way of integration "suggest that when we discern the proper scope of [each science] and the proper scope of faith, our feelings of tension are released. Nothing in science or faith has to be given up so as to release the tension; only something in our understanding of them, specifically, in our understanding of the proper scope of their claims."[15] Many people of faith and of science will hold to such a view. However, it is not always easy, in practice, to separate very strictly these two large dimensions of life.

---

13. Wolterstorff, *Educating for Shalom*, p. 38.

14. Ibid., p. 38

15. Ibid., p. 39.

Even after this brief presentation we can say that none of the three models, taken singularly, represent the best solution for a proper and authentic integration. It is, probably, safe to say that there are elements in each model that will apply when trying to do a proper dialogue between faith and science, between faith and learning.

A Christian University

When one speaks about a *Christian* university there are several questions that come to one's mind: Could such a project bring any contribution to the contemporary dialogue on the idea of 'university'? Is there a particular Christian input, a better way forward in higher education? Is there a specific vision or ultimate goal of higher education from a Christian perspective? Allow me to state here that there are many Christian scholars who analyze carefully these questions and offer affirmative answers pointing to several elements of a distinctly Christian contribution to higher education among which are the following: the communitarian character of Christian learning; the real interdependence of the agents in the overall process of education; a range of theologically shaped practices and virtues which aim at, and contribute to, authentic human flourishing; an hermeneutic of charity and an epistemology of love; an integrative understanding of the world and a vision of the unity of truth; delight, trust, and hope rather than doubt and suspicion; hospitality, vocation and worship as the context of learning.[16]

In a Christian vision of higher education the goal is not simply a particular way of thinking, though that is also true, but ultimately, "to equip and energize students for a certain way of being in the world . . . a Christian way . . . to pray and struggle for *shalom* [peace], celebrating its presence and mourning its absence."[17] To be sure, for such an education one needs to offer a particular kind of pedagogy and curriculum.

---

16. See particularly Douglas V. Henry and Michael D. Beaty, eds., *Christianity and the Soul of the University: Faith as a Foundation for Intellectual Community* (Grand Rapids: Baker Academic, 2006), pp. 10–15. For the most significant books addressing this question see the bibliographical list at the end of the article.

17. Wolterstorff, *Educating for Shalom*, p. 97.

Wolterstroff, for example, suggests three things that are central for such a goal in education.[18] First, since students come already shaped by the way of thinking and action of the dominant culture – capitalism, nationalism, and religious pluralism, the ideologies of progress, of individualism, and of our modern turn to the world – we must first enable them to arrive at a point of critical involvement, to help them loosen the grip of these things on them and to be able to hold up these practices and ideologies to the scrutiny of the biblical story. Second, the students need to be exposed to alternative ways of thinking, and motivated and energized for alternative ways of living. Instead of taking for granted the established structures and norms of various professions or occupations in modern society, we should stand back and inquire afresh about the real and ultimate goals as well as the appropriate norms for law, medicine, business, education, etc. The response should not be a posture of 'regressive romanticism', a returning back to what it was, but rather "we must struggle to see to it that no one of these sectors dominates our life as a whole – that our life together does not become economized or politicized or whatever; and that each sector pursues goals leading to health rather than illness."[19]

The third crucial aspect in Christian education is a concern for local and global justice! The preoccupation that everyone, including the marginalized, is not simply protected against any form of oppression but that she has a clear voice in the community. The students need to be made conscious of their own role and contribution to the life of society, to be encouraged for energized action and engagement in praxis-oriented theory. Christian education is thus education for life and not just for thought. In education understood this way, one speaks of 'radical conversion', of empathy, of one's whole way of life (not simply of individual actions), of joy, of wellbeing, of reconciliation, of peace. These will be some of the distinctively Christian features of a higher education that is shaped by the biblical story of a triune God who is totally committed to the ultimate human flourishing and actively engaged in the redemption of the world.

---

18. Ibid., pp. 97–99.
19. Ibid., p. 98.

Conclusion: Christian University and Postmodern Culture

In this short article I wanted to present the plausibility of a specifically Christian contribution to higher education and I hinted at several distinctive features. Of course, for a more comprehensive exposition and elaboration of this question, each of these elements presented above need to be analyzed, explored, and engaged with in a detailed and rigorous manner. My intention was only to show that religious based education has the potential for bringing a real contribution to the social arena and to name some features of a specifically Christian contribution.

Since Christian universities have existed for long time and will continue to function in the future, I would like to conclude my paper by briefly pointing out some important and relevant implications of pursuing the question of a *Christian* university's engagement with science and faith in a postmodern context.[20] I believe it is of utmost importance to begin with the need to have a solid Christian understanding of what represents a responsible belief. A serious reflection on the way we practice both science and faith will help us form such a belief. We have to uncover and nurture a religiosity that is conducive to human flourishing. Then, we have to recognize that in our interactions and dialogue with science we do that *as Christians*, from a particular historical, social and cultural context, from a distinctively Christian perspective – and this includes specific motivation and goals. For example, in the scientific inquiry a Christian will respect diversity, will be ready to change his or her mind on a specific issue when the evidence requires it, will understand that the goal of scholarship is not to be different from a non-Christian but will seek to be faithful to Scripture, to God and to the lordship of Christ.

A Christian university will attempt to be a place which develops and nourishes a community that will be able to engage fully with all areas of society, and critique any ethical values of the surrounding culture which are against an authentic human flourishing. The critical engagement with

---

20. For an excellent and elaborated discussion on this see "The Project of a Christian University in a Postmodern Culture" by Wolterstorff in his book *Educating for Shalom*, pp. 109–134.

culture, however, is shaped by the biblical narrative of hope – a narrative that presents human beings as being more than "producers and consumers of pleasure," and having a true hunger for ultimate meaning. Only such a narrative of hope will enable us to hear the cry of the destitute of the world and see the faces of those who endure suffering in any form. It will only be such confrontation with the tragic realities of our troubled world that will evoke in us the deepest form of love which will manifest itself in ethical actions of compassion, healing, restoration and reconciliation.

Finally, I would like to end this paper with a serious reminder issued by Scott Cunningham about the commodification of education, one of the clear directions towards which higher education in the west is moving. He rightly observes that "in Western higher education there is a fierce debate over the very purpose for a university education. Perhaps the most dominant value in Western culture is consumerism, meaning the value of the graduate is in either what she can produce or consume. In this view, education becomes crassly utilitarian. And, along with this, education becomes viewed and treated as a commodity."[21] It should be an important characteristic of Christian universities that they fight against this widespread tendency of commodification as this is against Christian values of integrity, honesty and the free inquiry for truth.

Bibliography

Bird, Darlene L. and Simon G. Smith, eds. *Theology and Religious Studies in Higher Education: Global Perspectives*. London/New York: Continuum, 2009.

Budde, Michael L. and John Wright, eds. *Conflicting Allegiances: the Church-Based University in a Liberal Democratic Society*. Grand Rapids: Brazos Press, 2004.

Constantineanu, Corneliu. *The Social Significance of Reconciliation in Paul's Theology: Narrative Readings in Romans*. London/New York: Continuum, 2010.

Dovre, Paul J., ed. *The Future of Religious Colleges*. Grand Rapids: Eerdmans, 2002.

---

21. Scott Cunningham, "The Future of Theological Education," *The Theological Educator* (2011), p. 9.

Gallagher, Tom. *Theft of a Nation: Romania Since Communism*. London: C. Hearst & Co, 2004.

Heie, Harold and David L. Wolfe, eds. *The Reality of Christian Learning*. Grand Rapids: Eerdmans, 1987.

Henry, Douglas V. and Michael D. Beaty, eds. *Christianity and the Soul of the University: Faith as a Foundation for Intellectual Community*. Grand Rapids: Baker Academic, 2006.

Henry, Douglas V. and Bob R. Agee, eds. *Faithful Learning and the Christian Scholarly Vocation*. Grand Rapids: Eerdmans, 2003.

Holmes, Arthur F. *Building the Christian Academy*. Grand Rapids: Eerdmans, 2001.

———. *The Idea of a Christian College*, Grand Rapids: Eerdmans, 1975.

Klassen, Norman and Jens Zimmermann. *The Passionate Intellect: Incarnational Humanism and the Future of University Education*. Grand Rapids: Baker Academic, 2006.

Liftin, Daune. *Conceiving the Christian College*. Grand Rapids: Eerdmans, 2004.

Mahoney, Kathleen A., J. Schmalzbauer and James Youniss. *Revitalizing Religion in the Academy*. Chesntnut Hill: Boston College Press, 2000.

Noll, Mark A. and James Turner. Thomas Albert Howard, ed. *The Future of Christian Learning: An Evangelical and Catholic Dialogue*. Grand Rapids: Brazos Press, 2008.

Pae, Harry Lee. *Christianity in the Academy: Teaching at the Intersection of Faith and Leaning*, Grand Rapids: Baker Academic, 2004.

Ringenberg, William C. *The Christian College: A History of Protestant Higher Education in America*, 2nd ed. Grand Rapids: Baker Academic, 2006.

Rogobete, Silviu. "Between Fundamentalism and Secularization: the Place and the Role of Religion in Post-Communist Orthodox Romania," in *Religion and Democracy in Moldova*, edited by S. Devetak, O. Sirbu and S. Rogobete. Maribor/Chisinau: ISCOMET/ASER, 2005.

Scott, David. *The Mind of Christ*. London/New York: Continuum, 2007.

Van Engen, John, ed. *Educating People of Faith: Exploring the History of Jewish and Christian Communities*, Grand Rapids: Eerdmans, 2004.

Ward, Graham and Michael Hoelzl, eds. *The New Visibility of Religion: Studies in Religion and Cultural Hermeneutics*. London/New York: Continuum, 2008.

Wolterstorff, Nicholas, Clarence W. Joldersma and Gloria Goris Stronks, eds. *Educating for Shalom: Essays on Christian Higher Education* Grand Rapids: Eerdmans, 2004.

CHAPTER 9

Choosing from Theology, *theology*, theology, and THEOLOGY: A Plea against Pigeonholing Theology in Universities

Corneliu C. Simuţ

This paper follows critically the argument of Professor William D. Hart (Hart, 2002) – professor of religious studies at the University of North Carolina, Greensboro, NC, USA – who believes that the academic study of religion should exclude certain perspectives on theology. He does not exclude theology as a discipline, but he makes some distinctions that point to various types of theology, some of which can be allowed to function within the academic study of religion, while others should be left aside or pursued in different contexts. For instance, he differentiates between Theology (with capital T) and *theology* (without capital T but with italics), in which Theology points to traditional, ecclesiastical approaches to theology (with confessional and dogmatic overtones) and *theology* designates a liberal reading of theology (with academic, humanistic, and philosophical preoccupations). He also uses theology (without capital T and without italics) to convey the idea of a neutral approach. In this paper, I shall express my disagreement with Professor Hart's model which is based on the distinction between Theology and *theology*, and favours the latter as a proper solution for what he calls a 'post-Theological culture'. My criticism is based on what I consider to be a fourth possibility which excludes all the three readings of theology proposed by Professor Hart (Theology, *theology*, and theology) in order to build on THEOLOGY (with capital letters). This model is neither ecclesiastical nor liberal, but fundamentally devotional, open, and academic.

Who is Afraid of Theologians?

Professor Hart's argument is captivating from the start for at least two reasons. First, it uses sexual imagery not only in its opening paragraph but also in other places, which are key for what he wants to convey. Second, it makes a clear distinction between various types of meanings attached to the concept of theology.

Hart is almost surgically precise in cutting through various understandings of the idea of theology. Before scientifically wielding his academic scalpel on the very body of theology, however, he artistically pictures a rather vividly sexual image of the protagonists. Religion in higher education is like a house, Hart explains, which has beds and bedfellows. Both the beds and the bedfellows are 'strange' in a sense: "The house of religious studies is full of strange beds and even stranger bedfellows. One often finds oneself in a strange bed, embraced by a stranger, not knowing how one got there and how to get out."[1] Hart compares the awkwardness and confusion of such a real life situation with the realm of religious studies where certain people may find themselves in similar situations when they do not know how to react to each other or how to distance from one another.

Hart rapidly identifies the root of the problem in the existence of two conflicting entities which he calls "the scholarly self and the dogmatic other". According to him, the scholarly self should be kept as far away as possible from the dogmatic other. Hart's 'scholarly self' represents the rigorously academic investigation of religion, while the 'dogmatic other' is defined as "an ecclesiastical agenda in the guise of scholarship". Hart's

---

1. Hart, William D., "From Theology to theology: The Place of 'God-Talk' in Religious Studies", in Linell E. Cady and Delwin Brown, eds., *Religious Studies, Theology, and the University: Conflicting Maps, Changing Terrain* (Albany, NY: State University of New York Press, 2002), pp. 93–109, p. 93.

intention to keep the two separate is so determined that he even advocates the necessity that a boundary should be set between them:

> For when this boundary is blurred, there can be a dreadful and palpable sense of violation. I use this sexually inflected term because being forced into a bed that one finds undesirable is still the privileged way of talking about such matters in this culture. This sense of violation may provide a useful account of why some in religious studies want to separate themselves from theologians.[2]

To his credit, Hart attempts to be fair to both parties involved in this academic conflict, but he cannot help siding with those in religious studies to the detriment of theologians. This is why the picture one gets from Hart is that of religious scholars being violated by theologians and, although he does not explicitly say that, the evident implication is that theologians are the violators while religious scholars appear to be some sort of innocent academic victims. The main problem, however, seems to be the reality of the church which, based on what can be inferred from Hart's general arguments, lurks behind the activity of theologians in the academy and causes distress among religious scholars to the point that the latter feel violated.

Hart, in his presentation of the problem, makes an effort to maintain a neuter position between religious scholars, such as himself, and theologians. In doing so, Hart defines religious scholars who are afraid of theologians as 'Victorians', some sort of 'stiff upper lip' academics who want to be dissociated from theologians because, if perceived as 'sleeping with theologians' as it were, they would have to face charges of intellectual promiscuity. His sexual imagery is detailed when he writes:

> These intellectual Victorians (bourgeoisie who are so easily shocked!) want to guard their chastity. They fear being caught with their pants down, of charges that they consort

---

2. Hart, "From Theology", p. 93.

with the wrong crowd. For these Victorians, to be caught in the company of a historian of religions is a venial sin and to be caught with a theologian is a mortal sin. Besides, don't they risk madness by engaging in these unnatural relations? What are respectable academics to think? Imagine the gossip, raised eyebrows, and the sardonic laughter. Imagine scientists and humanists, already suspicious of the academic study of religion, saying, "And these people think they belong in the arts and sciences?"[3]

In the end, it is all a matter of how today's culture works, because it is "in this culture", as Hart writes, that this fear of theologians is being manifested in higher education, most likely because it is associated with a wide range of presuppositions which – wrong or not – do cause religious scholars to stay away from theologians. The key word that seems to trigger this particular fear of theologians is 'church', so it is rather the theologians' ecclesiastical involvement which appears to create uneasiness within the academic camp of religious scholars. Why exactly this is the case may appear logical indeed, at least to Hart, since being in the church means adherence to certain doctrines and doctrines are constantly associated with bigotry, bigotry with narrow-mindedness, and narrow-mindedness with stupidity. Today's culture is afraid of organized religion(s) because today's people are literally afraid of the violence – verbal or even physical – associated with some particular institutional manifestations of certain religions. Thus, fear of institutional religion means fear of theology, namely of a more or less clearly defined set of beliefs which reportedly inflame the spirits of ardent believers; so there is a general fear of religious fanaticism which leads to what can be called, based on Hart's argument, a 'cultural fear' of theology.

---

3. Ibid., p. 93.

What is Theology?

Hart proceeds with a brief presentation of his methodology which attempts to be some sort of *via media* between the position of religious scholars who want to have nothing in common with theologians and the position of other academics who see no harm in putting the two together within the same departments in universities. Hart openly admits that he was 'tempted' indeed to jump in the camp of religious studies Victorians whose innermost academic convictions prompted them to sever theology from religious studies. However, he does not identify himself unambiguously as part of this intellectual party. Instead, he prefers to work with a neither-nor kind of methodology, which does not place him on the side of the religious studies Victorians and also keeps him at a safe distance from the opposite camp of those willing to shelter theology in the university.

Hart appears to sense that it would be intellectually wrong to detach theology from religious studies to the point that no relationship between the two exists any longer:

> I admit being tempted by the view that the intellectual health of religious studies demands that theology be strictly quarantined. But I am skeptical of this view as well. (. . .) I attempt to negotiate the tension between my temptation and my skepticism by exploring two interlocking questions: What is the relation between theology and religious studies? and Does theology have a place with religious studies? In response to these questions, I offer five theses. First, theology and religious studies, if not Siamese twins, are as closely related as mother and daughter; indeed, the former gave birth to the latter. Second, Theology has left powerful traces within the academic study of religion, which is evident in the way that religious studies departments are organized. Third, these Theological traces are a source of discontent. Fourth, standard ways of distinguishing theology from non-theological forms of religious studies fail. Fifth, while denying any role for

Theology within the academic study of religion, I argue that
the place of *theology* is secure.[4]

What is theology? Quite simply, it is the mother of religious studies and,
as often happens in real life, the mother and daughter belong to different
generations which means that it is not long before a conflict erupts between
the two. In its capacity of mother of religious studies, theology seems to
have only one fault, according to Hart, which is enough to send her away
from the academic venue of religious studies, and that is its traditional
character – as opposed, *bien sûr*, to the openly liberal approach favoured
by her daughter. When clinging to traditionalism and not with liberalism,
theology becomes Theology, a kind of 'God-Talk' which must be excluded
from the academy, Hart argues. Theology, he insists, cannot be accepted
in the academy as Theology because it is based on a certain confession of
faith, a clear set of dogmatic convictions, and it is always connected with
the reality of the church.

> I distinguish between Theology and *theology*. Theology with an
> uppercase 'T' refers to a devotional, confessional, and dogmatic
> enterprise, a professional, church-based enterprise; *theology*
> italicized with a lowercase 't' refers to a liberal, academic, and
> humanistic enterprise, a philosophical enterprise. Theology is
> fideistic; *theology* is fallibilistic. The former is absolutism born
> of skepticism. The latter is an open, revisable, hypothetical
> form of inquiry that rejects the either/or of absolutism and
> skepticism. I use theology, nonitalicized with a lower 't',
> to convey a meaning that is neutral between Theology and
> *theology* or where a distinction is not being made. (. . .) I
> comment *theology* to a post-Theological culture.[5]

Thus, according to Hart, devotion, confession, doctrine, and the church
cause harm to the cause of the academic study of religion. Only *theology*

---

4. Ibid., pp. 93–94.
5. Ibid., p. 94.

(with italics) can be accepted because this is not affiliated with any church and it is predominantly humanistic, philosophical, and academic; in a word, it is liberal, not traditional. Traditional Theology, as Hart puts it, promotes absolute beliefs and values which develop a certain type of skepticism towards other beliefs and values; for this reason there should be no place for it in the academic study of religion. Only *theology*, which is 'open', 'revisable' and 'hypothetical', can be accepted in the academy because it leads to the rejection of 'absolutism and skepticism'. Consequently, Hart proposes *theology* as the solution to what he calls a 'post-Theological culture', a mindset which is no longer willing to accept absolutes in anything, be it personal faith and values, communal belief and morality, or – even more so – academic convictions and expressions.

As far as Hart is concerned, the academy seems to have no room for a personalized theological conviction that may cling to beliefs in supernatural realities; theology must never be Theology but *theology*. Hart recommends liberal *theology* in a way which – according to his own confession – resembles Derrida's preference for a philosophy that is not heterologous, so it rejects the idea of the absolute Other. Derrida deals with his perspective on heterology especially in connection with his critical understanding of Levinas, who promotes a radicalization of the infinite exteriority of the Other.[6] Hart also defends Rorty's separation of Philosophy and philosophy, of which only the latter is to be accepted in a 'post-Philosophical culture'. Rorty's 'post-Philosophical culture' refers to a world no longer dominated by philosophy, but rather by literature which inspires people to seek literary models, while philosophical ideas are repudiated. This leads to a specific intellectual reality in which no discipline is considered the foundation for other disciplines.[7]

---

6. Derrida, Jacques, *Writing and Difference* (Chicago, IL: University of Chicago Press, 1978), pp. 93–95. Boothroyd, David, "Responding to Levinas", in Robert Bernasconi and David Wood, eds., *The Provocation of Levinas: Rethinking the Other* (London: Routledge, 1988), pp. 15–31, p. 27.

7. Hart, 2002, p. 94. Rorty, Richard, *Philosophy and the Mirror of Nature* (Princeton, NJ: Princeton University Press, 1979), p. 6. Williams, Michael, *"Rorty and the Knowledge of Truth"*, in Charles Guignon and David R. Hiley, eds., *Richard Rorty* (Cambridge: Cambridge University Press, 2003), pp. 61–80, p. 75.

It is quite clear that Hart does not like the distinction between the Same and the Other (in his case the 'scholarly Self' and the 'dogmatic Other'), which in theology translates into the differentiation between man as a created, natural, and material being on the one hand, and God as uncreated, supernatural, and spiritual being on the other. For Hart, man and God should overlap to the point of total coincidence, so that only a humanistic and liberal understanding of theology as *theology* prevails.[8]

Hart's solution, however, is unsatisfying. He seems to work with the assumption that theological studies advocate the ultimate truth of the church – hence the idea that theology lacks impartiality and claims some sort of epistemic privilege – while religious studies are totally impartial and disinterested.[9] He neglects the fact that religious communities continuously influence the spiritual, dogmatic, and ethical meanings of their religious traditions,[10] thus, the church does not necessarily promote a static narrow-minded position. Therefore, one may assume that the traditionalism of Theology, which is confessional, can be combined with the openness of *theology* (although not with its fundamental liberalism). This new approach, which I call THEOLOGY (uppercase all the way through), is non-confessional (i.e. not defending a particular confessional stance, even if the lecturer has one), but devotional, personal, and academic at the same time.

Why Pigeonholing Theology?

We should pigeonhole Theology, quite simply, to avoid rigidity, dogmatism, and therefore nonsense – this would be Hart's basic answer. Theology, Hart argues, belongs to "Bible colleges, seminaries, and divinity schools"

---

8. Hart, "From Theology", p. 94.

9. An assumption which is critically assessed by Francis Schüssler Fiorenza, "Theological and Religious Studies: The Contest of the Faculties", in Barbara G. Wheeler and William E. Farley, eds., *Shifting Boundaries: Contextual Approaches to the Structure of Theological Education* (Louisville, KY: Westminster/John Knox Press, 1991), pp. 124–125.

10. The American Academy of Religion "The Religious Studies Major and Liberal Education", in *Liberal Education* (2009) v. 95, issue 2, pp. 48–55.

because it is essentially a "Christian and church-based endeavour", so it is therefore exclusivistic.

What Hart seems to miss in his argument, however, is the fact that while theology can be exclusivistic dogmatically, it can be studied pluralistically, (i.e. different theological convictions can peacefully coexist in the academic sphere and can be studied side by side in the same department).

Another issue is that Hart refuses the academic acceptance of Theology because of its supposed rigidity and dogmatism. However, traditional Theology, with its 'rigidity' and 'dogmatism' should be studied academically not only in confessional schools, but also in religious departments. If it is really as bad as Hart claims (bad in the sense of harmful to the academic study of religion), then students should be fully aware of its theoretical tenets and practical manifestations (and perhaps even the possible threats it may or may not pose to society). This is why, in my opinion, pigeonholing theology in the academic study of religion may actually run against an informed apprehension of theology with its multifaceted teachings, practical manifestations, and complex history.

To his credit, Hart does encourage the study of theology as history, even within the academic study of religion but it is very unlikely that students will make proper sense of theology if studied exclusively from a historical standpoint. Regardless of whether they are rigid or immovable or even narrow-minded to the point that they make no sense to the secularized mind of a religious scholar, doctrines are utterly important for a decent understanding of theology from a purely intellectual perspective. Hart, however, is adamant in his conviction that the academic study of religion needs to work with a clear distinction between traditionalism and liberalism, dogmatism and openness, rigidity and freedom.

According to Hart, it is not as much the fault of Theology that it is traditional, dogmatic, and rigid; if blame is to be ascribed to anybody, then it is the religious community behind it – namely the church – that turned mere theology into Theology. This is why, in Hart's argument, theology must be detached from the restrictive and bigoted influence of religious communities in order to be handed over to religious scholars, whose open-mindedness and superior thinking are the only means to transform the traditionalism of theology (or even Theology) in the liberalism of *theology*.

There is no place at all for constructive Theology in religious studies departments. But what about *theology*? Here we speak of a different animal altogether. That I have been forced to reject false arguments against the inclusion of *theology* in religious studies departments only heightens the importance of the issue (. . .): If *theology*, as I have argued, is open, revisable, and hypothetical inquiry into the nature of the divine, then it has a proper place within departments of religious studies, within the arts and sciences. To speak of *theology* as one methodology among others is to misspeak, for there is methodological difference between *theology* and the methodologies employed in the arts and sciences. *Theology* (with lowercase 't') is, among other things, a philosophical enterprise, a species of speculative metaphysics, an effort to give a hypothetical account of the nature of things. (. . .) Thus, I conclude that *theology* is a legitimate mode of inquiry within the methodological plurality of religious studies. It is a 'guess at the riddle', one among many hypotheses on an open road to inquiry.[11]

Hart, though, seems a bit too idealistic in his hopes to build departments of religious studies that have no connections with religious communities. The attempt to exclude religious communities from the study of religion is to ignore the complexities of religion as manifested in various social contexts. Truly understanding religion requires an interaction with the social context in which religion flourishes.[12]

---

11. Hart, "From Theology", 106–107.
12. See Segovia, Fernando F., "Racial and Ethnic Minorities in Biblical Studies", in Mark G. Brett, ed., *Ethnicity and the Bible* (Leiden: Brill 1996), pp. 469–492, p. 471.

Concluding Remarks: The God of Pigeonholed Theology

Hart suggests that traditional Theology has an agenda which is disguised in some church-related academic expressions and therefore it should not be allowed to function within departments of religious studies but rather in confessional universities. While there might be some truth in this, it is – I surmise – equally true that religious scholars have an agenda of their own in attempting to remove traditional Theology from the academic study of religion by promoting liberal *theology* as the only valid and legitimate expression of religious inquiry in the academy.[13] Hart himself seems to be annoyed by the church's belief in a God that he cannot tolerate. Instead, he prefers to focus on nature:

> I sometimes long for the day when we (and I mean everybody) stop speaking theologically, when God-talk in its hallowed and explanatory senses is as quaint as ether-talk (. . .). I think that it is better to speak of nature rather than God, of our necessary finitude as one species among others, of the natural contingencies that cast us into the world of foundlings, of landing in places that we could not anticipate, of coping with our environment as best we can. (. . .) Here we run into a matter of taste; thus where *theologians* (of the open, hypothetical, and inquiring type) speak of God, I speak of nature.[14]

A supernatural God who exists ontologically as a radically different Other and who changes one's entire life is not easy to swallow by the academics who prefer a natural god who allows for personal freedom of choice in all matters pertaining to human life.[15] Thus, I believe that Hart is

---

13. See Jensen, Tim, "Religious Studies. A Global View, Vision, and Mission", in *Religion*, (2009), v. 39, pp. 383–386, p. 384.

14. Hart, "From Theology", p. 103.

15. See Dick, Steven J., "Cosmotheology. Theological Implications of the New Universe", in Steven J. Dick, ed., *Many Worlds: The New Universe, Extraterrestrial Life, and the Theological Implications* (East Peoria, IL: Versa Press, 2000), pp. 191–210, p. 204.

not so much bothered by the traditional Theology's rigidity, immovability, or dogmatism as he is scared of theologians who literally put their trust in a supernatural God that shapes not only their spiritual values but also their practical morality. This is why I am convinced that at the heart of Hart's attempt to pigeonhole theology in separate 'items' such as Theology, *theology*, and theology (and especially the distinction between the first two) one can see his repulsion towards a certain image of God which he simply cannot accept; hence his aversion towards its inclusion in the academic study of religion.

This explains Hart's desire to pigeonhole theology in such a way that traditional Theology remains confined in confessional institutions of higher learning, while only liberal *theology* should be allowed to infiltrate in religious studies departments. The God of *theology* is an image which turns the supernatural God of traditional theology into a concept that should – and this is the best scenario – appeal to the mind of 'reasonable people', a god who is easy to swallow, not very difficult to understand, and certainly theoretical enough not to demand any dramatic reshaping of one's personal values and practical morality. A god that does not change one's life is a god which does not invade one's comfort zone; this is the god of liberal *theology*, so avidly defended by Hart as necessary for the academic study of religion. The easy-going god of liberal *theology*, which of course should be studied academically, is nothing but the deified expression of man's social concerns; it is a concept which, as Hart points out, provides humanity with "the 'titanic' image of 'daddy' written large on the cosmos as 'big-daddy'": As a religious studies scholar *qua* scientist, I may think that God is merely the deification of social life (. . .), a family romance between "mommy, daddy, and me". But this is only one (complex) candidate for truth among others.

It is interesting though to notice that while Hart does not accept a heterologous pattern of philosophical or religious thought (i.e. a pattern in which there is distinction between the Same and the Other, which in theology means that there is distinction between man and God), his understanding of what the academy should look like from the perspective of theology is indeed heterologous (or one may say dualistic). Thus, traditional, devotional, confessional, and ecclesiastical Theology should be 'imprisoned' (my quotation marks) in church-related institutions of higher learning, while liberal, open, scientific, and philosophical *theology* should be commended as the only rigorous method for the academic study of theology.

If one is to accept Hart's argument, then it follows that an earnest student of religion, who is interested in Christianity as religion at least as much as he focuses on Islam or Judaism as religions, will be deprived of a wide range of perspectives which belong to the theoretical and practical manifestations of Christianity. The students of theology will miss some of the most essential practical aspects of religion if theology is severed from the community, which confessionally supports and promotes it. At the end of the day, this is nothing but the most simple, common-sense explanation which intends to clarify why theology should never be pigeonholed in the academy: the student must never be left in the dark concerning anything (no matter how irrelevant it may appear to some) when it comes to the academic study of any subject, let alone such an important phenomenon as religion.

What is needed in the academy, therefore, is not Theology or *theology* but THEOLOGY. This mode of enquiry should not only leave aside the potentially flammable character of ecclesiastical confessionalism, which upsets religious scholars, but also avoid the humanistic influence of liberalism, which is not favoured by classical theologians.

Bibliography

Boothroyd, David. "Responding to Levinas", in: Robert Bernasconi and David Wood, eds. *The Provocation of Levinas: Rethinking the Other*. London: Routledge, 1988, pp. 15–31.

Derrida, Jacques. *Writing and Difference*. Chicago, IL: University of Chicago Press, 1978.

Dick, Steven J., "Cosmotheology. Theological Implications of the New Universe", in: Steven J. Dick, ed. *Many Worlds: The New Universe, Extraterrestrial Life, and the Theological Implications*. East Peoria, IL: Versa Press, 2000, pp. 191–210.

Fiorenza, Francis Schüssler. "Theological and Religious Studies: The Contest of the Faculties", in Barbara G. Wheeler and William E. Farley, eds. *Shifting*

Boundaries: Contextual Approaches to the Structure of Theological Education. Louisville, KY: Westminster/John Knox Press, 1991, pp. 124–125.

Hart, William D, "From Theology to theology: The Place of 'God-Talk' in Religious Studies", in Linell E. Cady and Delwin Brown, eds. *Religious Studies, Theology, and the University: Conflicting Maps, Changing Terrain.* Albany, New York: State University of New York Press, 2002, pp. 93–109.

Jensen, Tim. "Religious Studies. A Global View, Vision, and Mission", *Religion,* Vol 39, (2009): 383–386

Rorty, Richard. *Philosophy and the Mirror of Nature.* Princeton, NJ: Princeton University Press, 1979.

Segovia, Fernando F. "Racial and Ethnic Minorities in Biblical Studies", in Mark G. Brett, ed., *Ethnicity and the Bible.* Leiden: Brill, 1996, pp. 469–492.

The American Academy of Religion "The Religious Studies Major and Liberal Education", in *Liberal Education,* Vol 95, issue 2, (2009): 48–55.

Williams, Michael. *"Rorty and the Knowledge of Truth"*, in: Charles Guignon and David R. Hiley, eds. *Richard Rorty.* Cambridge: Cambridge University Press, 2003, pp. 61–80.

CHAPTER 10

Theological Education and Academia: A Convictional Theological Perspective on Evangelical Learning[1]

Parush R. Parushev

This paper considers first the apparent dichotomy between the seminary professional training for ministry, and the academic theological education aspiring to full recognition by the established academic standards of university communities. The main argument of the paper is that evangelical theological education has to be guided by a bi-focal vision: a) in service of strengthening the convictional identity of a faith community (through primary practices of informal and formal learning in faith communities); and b) in mission to the public university to educate the whole person (through secondary practices and teleological aims of academic theological education). Therefore, although both theological activities are intrinsically connected to the life of a community of faith, they should take place in two institutionally different settings.

---

1. The work on this paper was supported partly through the research project, "Symbolic Mediation of Wholeness in Western Orthodoxy", GAČR P401/11/168 and develops further an argument presented earlier in my paper "Towards Convictional Theological Education: Facing challenges of contextualisation, credibility and relevance", in *Theological Education as Mission* (Schwartzenfeld, Germany: Neufeld Verlag, 2005), ed. by Peter F. Penner, pp. 185–208.

The Challenge of Credibility and Relevance

Theological education strives to meet two conflicting demands: relevance to the life and ministry of faith communities; and credibility according to the established societal standards of quality education. In a widely circulated analysis Jim Plueddemann, a professor of intercultural studies at Trinity Evangelical Divinity School, Deerfield, Illinois, and the former International Director for SIM,[2] addresses the challenge of practical relevance and academic excellence in theological education.[3] His analysis, coming from a missionary perspective, is particularly relevant to the concerns of this research. In what follows I will briefly summarize and comment on Plueddemann's argument.

Plueddemann opens his discourse by stating that educators do have competing standards of excellence "controlled by implicit [and different] values which are not open to dialogue."[4] Value systems are organized along a continuum of educational philosophies between "emphases in universals at one pole and emphases on specifics at the other pole".[5] In other words, at the one pole are philosophies of 'top-down' education,[6] which one can associate with the Herbartian paradigm of modern education, with a stress on rational values, ideas, reason, absolutes, and the theoretical.[7]

---

2. Serving in Mission (formerly "Sudan Interior Mission") in Charlotte, North Carolina, USA. Dr Plueddemann served with SIM in different capacities from 1967 until 2003.

3. Jim Plueddemann, "The Challenges of Excellence in Theological Education, Back to Hot Topic", SIM 2003, circular paper presented at a series of seminars 1995–2003, last in Germany for the International Council of Accrediting Agencies and in Kenya for the Nairobi Fellowship of Theological Colleges, available through http://www.sicrieproject. org/excellence_in_theological_education.html, last access on 30 September 2013, and on request through the Archive of SIM (web-page http://www.sim.org/). My quotations refer to the electronic copy. Originally published as J. E. Plueddemann, "The Challenge of Excellence in Theological Education," in *Excellence and Renewal: Goals for Accreditation of Theological Institutions*, ed. by Robert L.Youngblood (Carlisle: Paternoster, 1989), pp. 1–14.

4. Plueddemann, "The Challenge of Excellence", 1.

5. Ibid.

6. The term 'top-down' has been introduced by Arthur Peacocke in his *Theology for a Scientific Age*, 2nd enlarged ed. (Minneapolis, MN: Fortress Press, 1993), ch. 9.

7. It is named after the educational system developed by the Austrian philosopher and pedagogue Johann Friedrich Herbart (1776–1841) and his followers. For the most recent overview and critical examination of Herbart's ideas in pedagogy, see Jan Hábl, "The Challenge of Komenský's Anthropological Teleology to Modern Czech Pedagogy",

At the other pole are philosophies that have a 'bottom-up' orientation by stressing the empirical, aesthetic, culturally relative and concrete specifics of the local grass-root context.[8] One may trace the origins of these educational philosophies to the pragmatist conceptualizations of the Progressive Education.[9] These two value systems are incompatible and run past by each other as a 'rail fence.'[10] Different value systems evidence themselves in different emphases in philosophy, theology, religious styles, educational theories, and standards of accreditation. The 'top-down' educational systems put the accent on credibility of the academically recognized teaching of ideas and assume primacy of theory over practice. Contrary, 'bottom-up' educational systems begin with a specific context and stress the relevance. There is an unavoidable discrepancy between these standards and purposes of educational systems. Plueddemann admits that for centuries "there has been an unhealthy split between theory and practice, between universals and specifics, between the rational and empirical, between content-centred and student-centred curricula, between Word- and Spirit-oriented theology, and between academic and professional standards of excellence in theological education."[11]

While in inevitable tension, these two types of educational systems must not be separated, the author insists. The key to the renewal of theological education is in connecting the two incompatible value systems by intentional efforts of integrating aims that will hold the opposites

---

PhD Dissertation, University of Wales via IBTS, Prague, ProQuest, UMI Dissertations Publishing, 2008, ISBN: 9781124714509, pp. 24–55 and 214–216. Cf. Norbert Hilgenheger, "Johann Friedrich Herbart (1776–1841)", *Prospects: the quarterly review of comparative education*, XXIII, no.3/4 (1993), pp. 649–664, available electronically on http://www.ibe.unesco.org/International/Publications/Thinkers/ThinkersPdf/herbarte.pdf, last accessed 15 September 2013.

8. On holism, 'top-down' and 'bottom-up' causality, see Nancey Murphy and George F. R. Ellis, *On the Moral Nature of the Universe: Theology, Cosmology, and Ethics* (Minneapolis, MN: Fortress Press, 1993), p. 4 and *passim*.

9. It was originally proposed by the American philosopher John Dewey (1859–1952) in his *The School and Society* (first published in 1899) in reaction to Herbartianism, drawing on the thought of German idealism and Continental romanticism. For a critical assessment of progressivist movement, see Hábl, "The Challenge of Komenský's Anthropological Teleology", pp. 56–95 and 217–220.

10. Plueddemann, "The Challenges of Excellence", 2. Plueddemann uses this metaphor to define the 'top-rail' rational value system and 'bottom-rail' practical value system.

11. Ibid., p. 4.

together as the fence posts connect the rails of the fence running parallel. Thus, Plueddemann's solution to the challenge of competing standards of (theological) education is the regular and intentional effort to bridge the unavoidable gap that separates them.

> While theological educators debate the lack of balance between the rails, a deeper problem is that the integrating fence posts are not intentional enough, not frequent enough, and often not connected to the top or bottom rails of the fence. Fence posts in theological education are intentional and regular efforts to compel interaction between the world of ideas and the world of senses, between absolutes and specifics, between theory and practice. These efforts must intentionally be built into both the aims and methods of education.[12]

Further in his paper the author reviews the characteristic educational methods of top-down and bottom-up educational systems. He concludes that a kind of purposeful synthesis of knowledge and experience should be achieved by bringing intentionality to bear on educational methodology. "In order to promote excellence in theological education, teaching methods must do three things: they must teach important knowledge, stimulate quality experience, and compel critical interaction between knowledge and experience."[13]

In the last part of his paper Plueddeman addresses briefly the accreditation of theological education and readily admits that there is never a value-neutral accreditation.[14] He outlines the different agenda behind the accreditation of the two divergent educational systems. He agrees that the credibility of the top-down systems is defined in terms of the scholarly credentials of the faculty and academic features of the institution (library, journals, solid knowledge-based course, etc.). Accreditation of the bottom-up systems is defined in criteria contributing to "the ability of the graduates

---

12. Ibid., p. 5.
13. Ibid., p. 7.
14. Ibid., pp. 7–8.

to do well in ministry."[15] The paper ends with a pessimistic assessment of the current state of theological education and with an exhortation. "Most theological education is ineffective. Renewal requires a paradigm shift, a whole new way of thinking about knowledge and experience, about theory and practice. This is the challenge of excellence in theological education."[16] The answer of how to face the challenge is left open to the readers to find.

While Plueddemann's analysis of the opposites is penetrating, his attempted synthesis is rather Platonic and implausible. Only forceful bolts of good intention can connect the two worlds of ideas and of practice. An organic holistic synthesis of the opposites is missing. Instead, 'bridging the gap' is left to the good will of the two warring educational camps. No wonder the proposals of this sort have never worked.

In the analysis of the incompatibility of the two value systems one may see a close parallel with conservative-liberal theological divides. The emphases of the first types of value systems are similar to conservative theology's rational foundationalism based on the sole authority of the universals of Scripture and of the factuality and precise epistemological representation of directly revealed religious truth. The emphases of the second type value systems come very close to liberal theology's immanentism, expressivism, and experiential foundationalism. The perception of meaning of any religious event cannot be separated from the performance of the event and is embodied in contextual and specific religious experience. It is not the purpose of this paper to get into the details of the conservative-liberal theological divide; it has been done extensively elsewhere.[17] It suffices to say that both types of foundationalism – epistemological and experiential – are

---

15. Ibid., p. 7. An example of differing accreditation standards is the set of educational criteria applied in many continental European countries, in which there is a clear difference of vocational and academic higher education.

16. Ibid., p. 8.

17. Conservative vs. liberal evangelical dichotomy is unbridgeable. For an extensive argument, see Nancey Murphy, *Beyond Liberalism and Fundamentalism: How Modern and Postmodern Philosophy Set the Theological Agenda*, The Rockwell Lecture Series (Valley Forge, PA: Trinity Press International, 1996), pp. 11–82. For a summary of the argument see her *Theology in a Postmoden Age*, The Nordenhaug Lectures 2003 (Prague, CZ: IBTS Publisher, 2003), pp. 7–23.

reductive and they do not mix and match.[18] Neither do the educational systems that are based on these philosophical theological premises.

This brings forward a number of corollary questions: Is theological education formative for the church's teaching? Or is the teaching of the church – the 'doctrine'[19] – the starting point of theological reflections and by necessity of the theological curriculum? In other words, who teaches whom? This series of questions brings me to the next point of my reflections concerning contextualization.

Challenges of Contextualization

Before moving further into the discussion about the nature of theological education, it is important to reflect on what theological education is about. There is a complex dynamic of doctrine (teaching, education) *of the church* and doctrinal theology (teaching, education) *for the church*. The home of the practice of doctrine and the sources of theological reflections are ultimately in the holistic life of the believing community, intertwined with Bible reading. While both of these activities (i.e. doctrinal theology and practice of doctrine) are legitimate in their own rights, they are interdependent and there is an important logical priority in the theological discourse that must not be overlooked.

James Wm. McClendon argues that doctrine should not be "manufactured by academic theologians to be marketed by churches or pastors," or teachers.[20] The church traditions existed and developed for centuries without being guided top-down by academic theologians. Rather, the practice of doctrinal theology, McClendon insists,

---

18. On the reductive nature of foundationalism, see Parush R. Parushev, "Convictional Perspectivism: A Constructive Proposal for Theological Response to Postmodern Conditions" in *Mission in Context: Explorations Inspired by J. Andrew Kirk*, ed. by John Currie and Cathy Ross (Farnham, England: Ashgate, 2012), 111–124 (pp. 112–115).

19. On Christian doctrine (teaching) as the primary practice of the church and on multi-facet verbal and non-verbal performances of the practice of church's teaching, see James Wm. McClendon, Jr., *Systematic Theology: Volume II: Doctrine*, republished with the new introduction by Curtis W. Freeman (Waco, TX: Baylor University Press, 2012; originally published in 1994 by Abingdon Press), pp. 23ff.

20. Ibid, p. 24.

is secondary to church practice inasmuch as from Christian point of view it need not exist, cannot Christianly exist, save in service to the other. It presupposes the church practice, investigates it, seeks to assist it. Being a consultant and helper, it may not substitute itself for or guarantee the primary practice [of church's doctrine].

To put the point linguistically, the surface grammar of doctrinal theology may take various shapes: first-person confessions, historic descriptions of church teaching, axioms or theses derived from an organising principle, biblical exegesis, rhetoric ukases. Yet its deep structure is that of a grammar of persuasion seeking assent: It says, "This is what your present convictions appear (on such and such evidence) to be; this is what (for such and such reason) they appear to mean. Would it be better then (for considerations here presented) to transform these present convictions *thus*?" In such a servant's question, such 'thus?' all theology's first-person confessions, all its axioms and principles, all its arguments find their reason for being.[21]

In other words in the relationship of the church with its theological educational superstructure, the vector of teaching has its primary focal point in the church and points to academia not the inverse. However, while assuming and accepting the logical priority in practicing doctrine or of primary over the secondary levels of theological discourse, it is fair to say that any church concerned with its doctrine is in urgent and never ending need of theological service and, thus, in need of theological education. At this point two important considerations must be taken into account.

---

21. Ibid., p. 47. On Orthodox theological discourse, as an example of an organic theologizing, see John Meyendorff, *Bysantine Theology: Historical Trends and Doctrinal Themes*, reprint from the revised second edition (New York: Fordham University Press 1983; originally published in 1974, second edition 1979), pp. 4–7. Cf. Meyendorff's notion of 'churchly theology' in the chapter on "The Catholicity of the Church" in his *Living Tradition: Orthodox Witness in the Contemporary World* (Crestwood, NY: St. Vladimir's Seminary Press, 1978), p. 82.

First, for the service to be provided there should be a home for the community of theological discourse, which is the theological institution. The practice of theological doctrine is a hard work and it requires trained practitioners and experts in proper exercise and advancement of the practice. Turning again to McClendon's linguistic metaphor, developing the grammar of doctrinal theology presupposes utilizing the intellectual grammar of academic, critically reflective philosophical language of the culture. Passing the baton from one generation of theologians for the church to another is a cumulative and corporate process with its own integrity and peer supervision. This is theological education for the thick community of faith,[22] shaping the identity of those belonging to it. It may be expected that the 'accreditation' of the credentials of any 'thick' educational endeavour should be done primarily in and by the community of faith and its auxiliary structures (informal educational forums, associations, consortia networks of educational institutions, peer based accrediting associations, etc.). I call this the 'home mission' of theological education.

Second, I agree with the understanding of theology as 'a science of convictions', proposed by McClendon and James M. Smith. In their view theology is "the discovery, examination, and transformation of the conviction set of a given convictional community, carried on with a view to discovering and modifying the relation of the member convictions to one another, to other (nonconvictional) beliefs held by the community, and to whatever else there is."[23] In that understanding, the theological task cannot be confined to and compartmentalized inside the church only. It has to take into account 'whatever else there is'. Inevitably then theological education has another mission focus and another vector pointing beyond the church community to the world. It has the task not only to borrow and

---

22. 'Thin' community is a virtue (or vice) excelling community. It is held together by a limited range of specific interest (e.g. a community of musicians or of academic theologians). 'Thick' communities are story-formed through shared life and communal language within a particular social reality. On thick and thin communities, see Parush R. Parushev, "Gathered, Gathering, Porous: Reflections on the nature of baptistic community", *Baptistic Theologies*, 5:1 (Spring 2013), pp. 35–52, p. 37.

23. James Wm. McClendon, Jr. and James M. Smith, *Convictions: Defusing Religious Relativism,* revised and enlarged edition (Valley Forge, PN: Trinity Press International, 1994), p. 184 (originally published as *Understanding Religious Convictions* in 1975 by University of Notre Dame Press).

(properly) use culture's intellectual tools but also to engage the culture in a meaningful convictional discourse. To fulfil this role theological education has to provide a platform for participation in the 'thin' community of academic and public discourse, holding the participants in the limited interests of academic pursuits according to the rules and practices of the theological game.[24] Theology has a crucially important missionary task to the university as to any other culture.[25] In the public market of ideas, doctrinal theology has to provide for the visibility and intellectual credibility of the community of faith among other communities of faith (or of reason alone). Theology has a role to play in public universities either by individual Christian's witness[26] or by conscious attempt to regain its place in the university. "[T]heology had been central to the work of the university at its origin, and remains central even now."[27] But if this is true, theological education is called to play the fair game by acquiring the best of the public university's standards, including the willingness to submit to the standards of scrutiny of the academic credentials (with all of the worries which Plueddemann is rightly concerned). I call this the 'foreign mission' of theological education.[28]

---

24. On differing rules of the game, see Basil Mitchel's insightful essay "How to Play Theological Ping-Pong", in the collection of his *How to Play Theological Ping-Pong and Other Essays on Faith and Reason*, edited by William J. Abraham and Robert W. Prevost (Grand Rapids, MI: William B. Eerdmans Co., 1990), pp. 166–183. On rules of the practice of doctrine, see McClendon's *Doctrine*, pp. 21–62, cf. his *Systematic Theology: Volume I: Ethics*, republished from the revised edition with the new introduction by Curtis W. Freeman (Waco, TX: Baylor University Press, 2012; revised edition published 2002; originally published in 1986 by Abingdon Press), pp. 169–82.

25. "University is a culture. It organizes a set of cultural practices that enables the students to experience over time what can be experienced over time . . ." Chris Anderson, *Teaching as Believing: Faith in the University*, Studies in Religion and Higher Education Series, 2 (Waco, TX: Baylor University Press, 2004), p. 161.

26. See Chris Anderson's wonderfully written account of devote Christian in public university, Ibid., *passim.*

27. James Wm. McClendon, Jr., *Systematic Theology: Volume III: Witness*, republished with the new introduction by Curtis W. Freeman (Waco, TX: Baylor University Press, 2012; originally published in 2000 by Abingdon Press), p. 398.

28. For detailed analyses of complex arguments for the accreditation of theological education by specifically evangelical accrediting bodies over against accreditation by established or state recognized accreditation commissions, particularly in the context of the emerging evangelical educational institutions in the former Soviet Block countries, see David P. Bohn, "The Perspective on Theological Education Evident among Evangelical Church Leaders in Bulgaria, Hungary, Romania, and Russia", PhD Dissertation, (Trinity

If my line of argument so far is correct, it is legitimate to differentiate between theology of the church (or of the 'thick' community of faith) and theology for the church developed at secular educational institutions by the 'thin' community of academic theologians. Instead of trying to connect them forcefully with post-bolts of the rail fence systems of education, as Plueddemann suggests, the church will do better seeking ways of organic synergy and co-operation between these two legitimate arms of the church's mission to its own community of faith and to the society at large.

Another way to think about theological education is to relate the mission of education to the larger debate about the relationship of the church to the church's environments. Moving away from the stereotypical 'Christ and culture' framework of the debate set by the epigones of H. Richard Niebuhr's typology, one may see different approaches to theological education as different convictional expressions of the church's (or faith community's) attitude to the culture. One may look first at the *theology of correlation* best expressed in the works of Paul Tillich. This is an important starting point, for Tillich "more than any other twentieth century theologian . . . is the heir . . . to the Protestant theology of the nineteenth century", who "led that theology into the twentieth century".[29] Moreover, his views and works are often considered to be the cornerstone of the theology of culture.[30] One may look next at Julian Hartt's *Theology of Prophetic Critique*. Hartt "seeks to establish the identity of Jesus Christ and the sufficiency of his work by an analysis of Scripture's narrative". He speaks about the door open wide for us to participate in the Kingdom of God; about love's role, which turns

---

Evangelical Divinity School, 1997); Miriam L. Charter, "Theological Education for New Protestant Churches of Russia: Indigenous Judgments on the Appropriateness of Educational Methods and Styles", PhD Dissertation, (Trinity Evangelical Divinity School, 1997); Peter Penner, *Nauchite vse narody …: Missiya bogoslovskogo obrazovaniya* [Make disciples of all nations …: Mission of Theological Education] (St. Petersburg: "Biblia dlya Vseh", 1999, in Russian), pp. 157–187; a number of articles in the collection edited by Peter F. Penner, *Theological Education as Mission* (Schwartzenfeld, Germany: Neufeld Verlag, 2005); Scott D. Edgar, "Pastoral Training among Baptist in Ukraine: Conversation between indigenous voices and theoretical perspectives", PhD Dissertation, (University of Wales via IBTS, 2007).

29. McClendon, *Witness*, p. 39.

30. See his *Theology of Culture*, edited by Robert C. Kimball (New York, NY: Oxford University Press, 1959).

away from the old cultural pattern, to the New Kingdom.[31] Finally, one may wish to visit John Howard Yoder's holistic *whole New World (new creation in Christ) theology.* The beginning point of the discussion of Yoder's theology, perhaps, will be his understanding that Jesus in his original setting, in his radical demand for justice, peacemaking and discipleship, should be the norm for Christian ethics and witness.[32] Or for the best, one must keep in unity all perspectives outlined above:

> In transmitting the Great Story, the church must be alert to openings, hungers, hidden religious depths within the contemporary culture (thus Tillich). Even more must it become aware by the light of that long narrative of the illusions and self-deceit of the culture-world, so that its preaching enables the world rightly to see itself (thus Hartt) . . . [And] the church must be not only the preacher but also the present instance of the gospel of Jesus Christ (thus Yoder).[33]

Thus, what the church (and its theological institutions) needs today is a blend of these different theological perspectives, a construct that relates harmoniously their best parts with integrity. The church must be able to understand society, must be able to hear and be open to its needs and concerns. At the same time it should not abandon its prophetic role of exposing sins and vices of the world. The church's critique is legitimate only when the church practices what it preaches.

---

31. McClendon, *Witness*, pp. 43–44. See Hartt's *A Christian Critique of American Culture: An Essay in Practical Theology* (New York, NY: Harper & Row, 1967). Cf. Jonathan R. Wilson, *Theology as Cultural Critique: The Achievement of Julian Hartt*, Studies in American Hermeneutics Series, 12 (Macon, GA: Mercer University Press, 1996).

32. See his *The Politics of Jesus: Behold the Man! Our Victorious Lamb*, 2nd edition (Grand Rapids, MI: William B. Eerdmans/ Carlisle, UK: Paternoster, 1994, 1972).

33. McClendon, *Witness*, p. 49. For relating McClendon's analysis to the realties of post-communist Europe, see Lina Andronoviene and Parush R. Parushev, "Church, State, and Culture: On the Complexities of Post-Soviet Evangelical Social Involvement", *Theological Reflections*, EAAA Journal of Theology, 3 (2004), 194–212 (with translation in Russian "Tserkov', Gosudarstvo i Obshchestvo: o slozhnosti uchastija postsovetskih evangel'skih hristian v zhizni obshchestva", *Bogoslovskie Razmishlenija*, 174–193; and Lithuanian "Bažnyčia, Valstibe ir Kultūra: apie evangelišku postsovietmečio bažnyčiu visuomeniškumo problematika", 213–227).

Education and Socialization

There is yet a third way of assessing the role of theological education, namely, in terms of socialization. Education is a primary means for socialization. It can be affirmative or subversive to one's identity. Biblical narrative presents different contexts of socialization. In the theocratic Hebrew society the vehicles of socialization were the extended family, the market place and the worshipping community gathered together in the Temple or in the synagogues. In the democracies and tyrannies of the Greco-Roman world encountered by Jewish and early Christian missionaries, these were the public baths, the coliseums, the amphitheatres and the schools of philosophical discourse at the public squares. The issues of beliefs and morals were hotly debated in the close circles of philosophers as much as at the trading lots of the merchants.[34] It is in this cultural milieu that the Jewish Diaspora and the emerging Christian communities took their roots, made themselves at home and, importantly, started developing their theological idioms.

There is an implicit sectarian syndrome hidden behind the notion of explicitly Christian (or religious) education for explicitly Christian (or religious) schools. In the world touched by the European civilization of the Enlightenment, the public school's classroom is still a place where socialization occurs and the public university is still the laboratory for intellectual maturity. These are learning paths of inquiring to become the citizen of the globalized world. Having accepted multi-culturalism, public universities are now facing yet another challenge – one of spirituality and realities of life beyond reason. It is the task of a Christian and of the Christian community in the university to help the university community accomplish its pluralistic mission of holistic teleological education of personhood.[35]

---

34. St. Gregory of Nazianzus complain "about salesmen discussing the concept of 'cosubstantial' in the market place," see Meyendorff, *Bysantine Theology*, p. 5.

35. My younger colleague Jan Hábl offered important insights into the usefulness of pre-modern holistic patterns of education for the post-modern cultural contexts. See his doctoral dissertation "The Challenge of Komenský's Anthropological Teleology to Modern Czech Pedagogy", in his book *Ultimate Human Goals in Comenius and Modern Pedagogy* (Hradec Kralove, Czech: Gaudeamus, 2011, in Czech) and his paper "Character

Christian education has to address this task head on by careful turning to the proper ends of education, discovering the right ways of being and hermeneutically appropriating the sacred texts as well as the texts of 'whatever else there is.'

Conclusion

Christian educators are faced with the complex task of the mission of theological education on three levels. Correspondingly, my colleague, David Brown defines the purpose of theological education in three symbolic pictures. These are the filling of 'the empty bottle' by transmitting trivial and yet necessary information; 'passing the baton' and training a person for the role of responsibility and accountability for the ministry in a particular faith community; and 'opening the door' to wider horizons of Christian vision and inspiration.[36]

'Filling a bottle' is a mission for identity formation in the life of the church. It is like growing a child in a family by passing on and affirming convictions of a particular believing community. Such education can be achieved by means of the primary theological level of engaging the practice of doctrine in first and foremost denominational Bible colleges, informal educational groups, and the like.

'Passing the baton' includes clarifying and building a platform for intimate conversations among diverse and yet spiritually closely-bound communities – something like speaking to the village of a 'kin' of 'the like-minded'. It has been my experience that national seminaries, schools of local unions and associations are becoming platforms of exchange – clarification of opinions for building a platform of denominational or intra-confessional dialogue. These are types of educational institutions for the service of larger

---

Formation: A Forgotten Theme of Comenius's Didactics", in *Journal of Education and Christian Belief*, 15:2 (Autumn 2011), 141–152 (available electronically onhttp://www. academia.edu/2008389/Character_Formation._A_Forgotten_Theme_of._Comeniuss_ Didactics, last accessed 15 September 2013).

36. "Theological Education: filling a bottle, passing a baton, opening a door," *Journal of European Baptist Studies*, 1:2 (January 2001), 5–20 (pp. 7–14).

homogeneous communities of faith or for interdenominational encounters. These undergraduate or professional graduate level institutions have a primary focus of educating the church in its local and associative sense.[37] They are called to pass on or clarify convictional identity by discerning, affirming or revising convictions and conviction sets of the 'kin'. They are the places of building common grounds for communal discernment for a family of faith and embodiment of pastoral spirituality in the life of a particular family of faith. Theirs is the task of enhancement of the gifts and calling for leadership and pastoral ministry discerned by gathering communities.[38] Unless required by specific circumstances beyond the educational objectives of the faith community, secular public accreditation is irrelevant to their successful mission and may do more harm than good.

Finally, theological education has a mission to the culture by 'opening the door' to reach out beyond the immediate concerns of a faith community. This 'dialogue' can be the witness of the lived-out faith and verbal witnessing in inter-confessional, pluralistic and public dialogue.[39] For that to happen, there is a need and a place for theological institutions aiming at opening a dialogue with other religious communions or the society at large. Here is where upper-level research master's and doctoral programme's place is, and here is where the accreditation and the relevance of education measured by the standards of secular academic structures is important. And here is where theological education addresses the culture on culture's own terms by building bridges and establishing alliances with the 'unlike-minded'.[40]

---

37. On the interdependency of local communities of faith even where they are not part of an institutional church, see Keith G. Jones, *The European Baptist Federation: A Case Study in European Baptist Interdependency 1950–2006* (Milton Keynes, England: Paternoster, 2009).

38. Keith G. Jones, "Spirituality and Structures", *Journal of European Baptist Studies*, 13:2 (January 2013), 29–49 (pp. 43–47) and Parushev, "Gathered, Gathering, Porous".

39. Here again the integrity of the living faith precedes and is the necessary condition for an authentic evangelistic engagement with the society. See Brad J. Kallenberg's *Live to Tell: Evangelism for a Postmodern Age* (Grand Rapids, MI: Brazos Press, 2002).

40. Parush R. Parushev, *Christianity in Europe: The way we are now,* with a response by Vija Herefoss, in the Crowther Centre Monographs Series, Volume 9 (Oxford: Church Missionary Society, 2009), pp. 4, 19.

Bibliography

Anderson, Chris. *Teaching as Believing: Faith in the University.* Studies in Religion and Higher Education Series, 2. Waco, TX: Baylor University Press, 2004.

Andronovienė, Lina and Parush R. Parushev. "Church, State, and Culture: On the Complexities of Post-Soviet Evangelical Social Involvement", *Theological Reflections,* EAAA Journal of Theology, 3 (2004): 194–212.

Bohn, David P. "The Perspective on Theological Education Evident among Evangelical Church Leaders in Bulgaria, Hungary, Romania, and Russia", PhD Dissertation, Trinity Evangelical Divinity School, 1997.

Brown, David. "Theological Education: filling a bottle, passing a baton, opening a door," *Journal of European Baptist Studies,* 1:2 (January 2001): 5–20.

Charter, Miriam L. "Theological Education for New Protestant Churches of Russia: Indigenous Judgments on the Appropriateness of Educational Methods and Styles", PhD Dissertation, Trinity Evangelical Divinity School, 1997.

Dewey, John. *The School and Society.* Chicago: University of Chicago Press, 1915. First published in 1899.

Edgar, Scott D. "Pastoral Training among Baptist in Ukraine: Conversation between indigenous voices and theoretical perspectives", PhD Dissertation, University of Wales via IBTS, 2007.

Hábl, Jan, "The Challenge of Komenský's Anthropological Teleology to Modern Czech Pedagogy", PhD Dissertation, University of Wales via IBTS, Prague, ProQuest, UMI Dissertations Publishing, 2008, pp. 24–55 and 214–216.

———. "Character Formation: A Forgotten Theme of Comenius's Didactics", *Journal of Education and Christian Belief,* 15:2 (Autumn 2011): 141–152. Available electronically on http://www.academia.edu/2008389/Character_Formation._A_Forgotten_Theme_of._Comeniuss_Didactics (Accessed on 15 September 2013).

Hartt, Julian. *A Christian Critique of American Culture: An Essay in Practical Theology.* New York: Harper & Row, 1967.

Hilgenheger, Norbert. "Johann Friedrich Herbart (1776–1841)", *Prospects: the quarterly review of comparative education,* XXIII, no.3/4 (1993), pp. 649–664. Available electronically on http://www.ibe.unesco.org/International/Publications/Thinkers/ThinkersPdf/herbarte.pdf, (Accessed on 15 September 2013).

Jones, Keith G. *The European Baptist Federation: A Case Study in European Baptist Interdependency 1950–2006.* Milton Keynes, England: Paternoster, 2009.

————. "Spirituality and Structures", *Journal of European Baptist Studies*, 13:2 (January 2013): 29–49.

Kallenberg, Brad J. *Live to Tell: Evangelism for a Postmodern Age*. Grand Rapids, Michigan: Brazos Press, 2002.

McClendon, James Wm., Jr. and James M. Smith. *Convictions: Defusing Religious Relativism*. Valley Forge, PN: Trinity Press International, 1994.

McClendon, James Wm., Jr. *Systematic Theology: Volume I: Ethics*, republished from the revised edition with the new introduction by Curtis W. Freeman. Waco, TX: Baylor University Press, 2012. Originally published in 1986 by Abingdon Press).

————. *Systematic Theology: Volume II: Doctrine*, republished with the new introduction by Curtis W. Freeman. Waco, TX: Baylor University Press, 2012. Originally published in 1994 by Abingdon Press.

Meyendorff, John. *Bysantine Theology: Historical Trends and Doctrinal Themes*. New York: Fordham University Press, 1983. Originally published in 1974.

————. *Living Tradition: Orthodox Witness in the Contemporary World*. Crestwood, New York: St. Vladimir's Seminary Press, 1978.

Mitchel, Basil. "How to Play Theological Ping-Pong," in: William J. Abraham and Robert W. Prevost, ed. *How to Play Theological Ping-Pong and Other Essays on Faith and Reason*. Grand Rapids, MI: William B. Eerdmans Co., 1990, pp. 166–183.

Murphy, Nancey and George F. R. Ellis. *On the Moral Nature of the Universe: Theology, Cosmology, and Ethics*. Minneapolis, MN: Fortress Press, 1993.

Murphy, Nancey. *Beyond Liberalism and Fundamentalism: How Modern and Postmodern Philosophy Set the Theological Agenda*, The Rockwell Lecture Series. Valley Forge, PA: Trinity Press International, 1996.

————. *Theology in a Postmoden Age*, The Nordenhaug Lectures 2003. Prague, CZ: IBTS Publisher, 2003.

Parushev, Parush R. "Towards Convictional Theological Education: Facing challenges of contextualisation, credibility and relevance", in: Peter F. Penner, ed. *Theological Education as Mission*. Schwartzenfeld, Germany: Neuefeld Verlag, 2005, pp. 185–208.

————. *Christianity in Europe: The way we are now*. With a response by Vija Herefoss, in the Crowther Centre Monographs Series, Volume 9 (May 2009). Oxford: Church Missionary Society, 2009.

————. "Convictional Perspectivism: A Constructive Proposal for Theological Response to Postmodern Conditions" in: John Curries and Cathy Ross, ed. *Mission in Context: Explorations Inspired by J. Andrew Kirk*. Farnham, England: Ashgate, 2012, pp. 112–115.

———. "Gathered, Gathering, Porous: Reflections on the nature of baptistic community", *Baptistic Theologies*, 5:1, (Spring 2013): 35–52.

Peacocke, Arthur. *Theology for a Scientific Age*. Minneapolis, MN: Fortress Press, 1993. 2nd enlarged ed.

Penner, Peter. *Nauchite vse narody …: Missiya bogoslovskogo obrazovaniya* [Make disciples of all nations …: Mission of Theological Education]. St. Petersburg: "Biblia dlya Vseh", 1999, in Russian.

———. *Theological Education as Mission*. Schwartzenfeld, Germany: Neuefeld Verlag, 2005.

Plueddemann, Jim. "The Challenges of Excellence in Theological Education, Back to Hot Topic", paper presented to the Nairobi Fellowship of Theological Colleges in Nairobi, Kenya, 10 July 1987. Available through http://www.sicrieproject.org/excellence_in_theological_education.html (Accessed on 30 September 2013).

Tillich, Paul. *Theology of Culture*. New York: Oxford University Press, 1959.

Wilson, Jonathan R. *Theology as Cultural Critique: The Achievement of Julian Hartt*, Studies in American Hermeneutics Series, 12. Macon, GA: Mercer University Press, 1996.

Yoder, John Howard. *The Politics of Jesus: Behold the Man! Our Victorious Lamb*. Grand Rapids, Michigan: William B. Eerdmans/ Carlisle, UK: Paternoster, 1994, 1972.

Contributor's Biographies

Rev Dr Tamás Béres is a university professor of Systematic Theology at the Lutheran Theological University in Budapest. Tamás wrote his PhD thesis on the role of myth in the theological work of Paul Tillich. Recently he defended his Habilitation thesis at Debrecen Reformed University, which was about ecotheology. For the past years he has addressed public theological questions in his professional activity.

Dóra Bernhardt has an MA in languages and a ThM from Regent College, Vancouver, BC. She is currently teaching at the Department of English at the Károli Gáspár University of the Reformed Church in Hungary and finishing her PhD studies at the Vrije Universiteit Amsterdam in Systematic Theology. She has acted as sessional lecturer at the Central and Eastern European Institute for Mission Studies.

Rev Dr Corneliu Constantineanu (PhD, University of Leeds and the Oxford Centre for Mission Studies, UK) is Professor of New Testament Studies and Rector of Theological Pentecostal Institute in Bucharest, Romania. He is the former Academic Dean of Evanđeoski teološki fakultet in Osijek, Croatia where he taught for more than 16 years, and also the former Executive Director of the Areopagus Centre for Christian Studies and Contemporary Culture in Timisoara, Romania. In addition to his specialization and publications in the areas of Pauline theology and reconciliation, Corneliu has a special interest in pursuing a holistic understanding of the gospel as public truth, thus trying to integrate Christian faith with cultural, social and political realities of everyday life.

Rev Dr Tamás Czövek is an ordained minister in the Reformed Church in Hungary. He did his Masters degree in Old Testament at Columbia Theological Seminary and his PhD with the Oxford Centre for Mission Studies. Currently he teaches Old Testament at the Pentecostal Seminary in Budapest.

Dr Tibor Fabiny is Professor of English Literature and Hermeneutics at Károli Gáspár University of the Reformed Church in Hungary where he is Head of the English Institute and Director of the Center for Hermeneutics including the Jonathan Edwards Center - Hungary. He is also a lay theologian, a member of the Lutheran Church in Hungary and the President of the Hungarian Luther Alliance. He has published books and articles widely on Christian Hermeneutics, the English Reformation and Literature of the 16th–17th Centuries.

Dr Ábrahám Kovács is an Associate Professor at Debrecen Reformed University. After obtaining his MTh from Princeton, he earned his PhD at the University of Edinburgh in 2003. He has published several books with Peter Lang and L'Harmattan Publishing House. Dr Kovács' articles focus on Christian theology, comparative theologies, mission studies, Jewish-Christian relations and Scottish Hungarian church history. He is trained as a historian, theologian and historian of religion.

Rev Dr András Lovas is senior pastor of Gazdagrét Reformed Church in Budapest, Hungary. He also mentors church planters and is involved in seminary training for urban ministry and church planting at Károli Gáspár Reformed University. András holds a Doctor of Ministry degree in missional leadership in the city, having graduated from Bakke Graduate University in 2006.

Dr Ksenija Magda, Doc Hab, is Professor of New Testament at the Theological Faculty 'Matthias Flacius Illyricus' in Zagreb, Croatia. Dr Magda completed her PhD at the London School of Theology (Brunel University) reading on Paul's Territoriality and Mission Strategy in the Epistle of Romans. The book was published in Germany by Mohr-Siebeck

Verlag. Dr Magda's interest is the reception of biblical texts in contemporary contexts. She has been involved in the ministry of the Croatian Baptist Union where she was the Director of the Baptist Institute of Adult Training in Faith and Doctrines for 10 years and the President of Baptist Women for 12 years. Dr Magda is currently serving as Chair of the Academic Committee of the Board of Trustees of the International Baptist Theological Study Centre (Amsterdam).

Rev Dr Parush R. Parushev, Doc Hab, (Bulgaria) is an ordained Baptist minister. He has doctoral degrees in applied mathematics (St Petersburg, Russia) and theology (Fuller, California) and Habilition in science and theology. Dr Parushev is currently the Rector and Dean of Research at the International Baptist Theological Seminary of the European Baptist Federation in Prague, Czech Republic. He is a senior lecturer in theology at IBTS and Free University Amsterdam and the founding Director of the Institute for Systematic Studies of Contextual Theologies (IBTS).

Rev Dr István Pásztori-Kupán, MTh, PhD, Doc Hab, is a Professor of Reformed Systematic Theology and History of Christian Doctrine at the Protestant Theological Institute in Kolozsvár (Cluj), Transylvania, Romania. He obtained his PhD at the University of Edinburgh in 2003 and his Habilitation at the Reformed Theological University in Debrecen in 2010. His publications include a monograph about Theodoret of Cyrus, a Greek theologian of the fifth century, published in The Early Church Fathers series by Routledge in 2006. www.proteo.hu/pasztori

Dr Zoltán Schwáb earned his PhD in Old Testament studies from Durham University where he is currently a teaching assistant. Before commencing his theological research focusing on Old Testament wisdom literature he worked as the General Secretary of the Hungarian Fellowship of Evangelical Students.

Dr Corneliu C. Simuţ is Professor of Historical and Systematic Theology at Emanuel University of Oradea, Romania. Professor Simuţ holds a PhD in Church History from the University of Aberdeen, a ThD in Dogmatic

Theology from the University of Tilburg, a Habilitation in Systematic Theology from the Reformed Theological University of Debrecen, and a DD (by publications) from the University of Pretoria. He is currently the Editor-in-Chief of Perichoresis, the theological journal of Emanuel University (published in conjunction with Walter de Gruyter Open), and has recently been appointed associate research fellow at the University of Pretoria.

Langham Literature and its imprints are a ministry of Langham Partnership.

Langham Partnership is a global fellowship working in pursuit of the vision God entrusted to its founder John Stott –

> *to facilitate the growth of the church in maturity and Christ-likeness*
> *through raising the standards of biblical preaching and teaching.*

Our vision is to see churches in the majority world equipped for mission and growing to maturity in Christ through the ministry of pastors and leaders who believe, teach and live by the Word of God.

Our mission is to strengthen the ministry of the Word of God through:

- nurturing national movements for biblical preaching
- fostering the creation and distribution of evangelical literature
- enhancing evangelical theological education

especially in countries where churches are under resourced.

Our ministry

Langham Preaching partners with national leaders to nurture indigenous biblical preaching movements for pastors and lay preachers all around the world. With the support of a team of trainers from many countries, a multi-level programme of seminars provides practical training, and is followed by a programme for training local facilitators. Local preachers' groups and national and regional networks ensure continuity and ongoing development, seeking to build vigorous movements committed to Bible exposition.

Langham Literature provides majority world pastors, scholars and seminary libraries with evangelical books and electronic resources through grants, discounts and distribution. The programme also fosters the creation of indigenous evangelical books for pastors in many languages, through training workshops for writers and editors, sponsored writing, translation, strengthening local evangelical publishing houses, and investment in major regional literature projects, such as one volume Bible commentaries like *The Africa Bible Commentary*.

Langham Scholars provides financial support for evangelical doctoral students from the majority world so that, when they return home, they may train pastors and other Christian leaders with sound, biblical and theological teaching. This programme equips those who equip others. Langham Scholars also works in partnership with majority world seminaries in strengthening evangelical theological education. A growing number of Langham Scholars study in high quality doctoral programmes in the majority world itself. As well as teaching the next generation of pastors, graduated Langham Scholars exercise significant influence through their writing and leadership.

To learn more about Langham Partnership and the work we do visit **langham.org**

Lightning Source UK Ltd.
Milton Keynes UK
UKOW04f2016240814

237443UK00008B/113/P